Volcanoes and Earthquakes

MODULE C

Volcanoes and Earthquakes

Do you judge the earth by its cover? If you do, you might not be aware of the powerful forces deep beneath the surface of the earth. In this module, you'll find out how these forces create volcanoes, start earthquakes, form mountains, and move continents.

CHAPTER 1 Beneath the Earth

Is the earth solid to the core? The layers of rock beneath the earth's crust are solid, liquid, and everywhere in between.

CHAPTER 2 Explosive Volcanoes

Kaboom! From time to time, one of the earth's many volcanoes erupts explosively, forming a cloud of gas, rocks, and ash.

CHAPTER 3 Faults and Quakes

Are you ready for the big one? Major earthquakes can cause incredible damage, but you can protect yourself by playing it safe.

Beneath the Earth

Sounds weird. What do you think it is?

What is indirect evidence?

Get a shoe box from your teacher. The shoe box contains a mystery object. Find out as much as you can about the mystery object. There is just one rule: you can't look inside the box. Record what you did. What did you learn about the mystery object?

For Discussion

1. How can you find the weight of the object?
2. Why is the information you found called indirect evidence?

Liquid Rocks

Do rocks melt?

The ground trembles. The earth cracks. The clock strikes twelve midnight. Just past midnight, on January 3, 1983, fountains of red-hot liquid begin spurting out of cracks along the eastern slope of Kilauea (kē′lou ā′ə), a volcano on the island of Hawaii.

The thick liquid—called **lava**— glows like the coals of a fire. The lava rises dozens of meters into the air, then falls back to the earth. Wherever the lava falls, it sears the ground with heat great enough to melt rocks. Meanwhile, foul-smelling gas spreads throughout the air and joins the smoke of burning trees and other plants.

The sun rises, and still the lava keeps spurting from the ground. But now it begins flowing away from the lava fountains and spreading outward across the sloping land. As the lava spreads, it starts to cool. Over time, large masses of lava harden into thick carpets of black rock. In between these black carpets, rivers of red-hot lava, like the ones in the picture, continue to flow.

Over the next three weeks, 14 million cubic meters of lava will spurt out of the ground, covering almost 5 square kilometers of land. And this will be just the beginning. Time and time again, the lava will rise out of the ground, covering more and more land. Where did all the lava come from, and where will it go? You'll find out in this chapter.

▼ *Lava erupts from Kilauea in Hawaii, and flows across the land.*

► The earth has three main layers: the core, the mantle, and the crust. The continents and islands are part of the crust. The core has two parts: the inner core and the outer core.

Into The Field

Which plate are you living on?

Find a map that shows the surface of the earth divided into plates. Draw the map and put an x where you live. Label the plate that you live on.

The Layers of the Earth

The earth is a slightly flattened sphere made of three major layers. The outer layer is called the crust. The middle layer is called the mantle. Some of the mantle is solid, some liquid. The inner layer is called the core.

The picture shows the three layers of the earth. The rocky crust covers the entire planet—from the top of the highest mountain to the floor of the deepest ocean. The rock that makes up the crust beneath the ocean is hard, black, and about 3 to 7 kilometers thick. The rock that makes up the crust of the continents is hard, coarse, and has many colors. This continental crust is usually thicker than the crust beneath the ocean.

The bottom of the earth's crust is much hotter than the surface. In its deepest parts, the crust is hot enough to melt some rocks. But, it's less than half as hot as the next layer, the mantle.

Like the crust, the mantle is mostly solid rock. But the mantle is far thicker and hotter than the crust. Silicon, oxygen, aluminum, and iron make up most of the rock in the mantle. The mantle is nearly 3000 kilometers thick.

The center of the earth, the core, is made of two parts. These parts are the inner core and the outer core. The outer core is made of melted iron and nickel. It is more than 2000 kilometers thick and hotter than the mantle. The inner core is a solid ball of white-hot iron and nickel. The distance from the edge to the middle of the inner core is about 1300 kilometers. The temperature of the inner core is even hotter than the temperature of the outer core.

The lava that spurted from Kilauea probably formed in the upper part of the earth's mantle. The temperature in the upper mantle is hot enough to melt some rock. Hot melted rock within the earth is called **magma.**

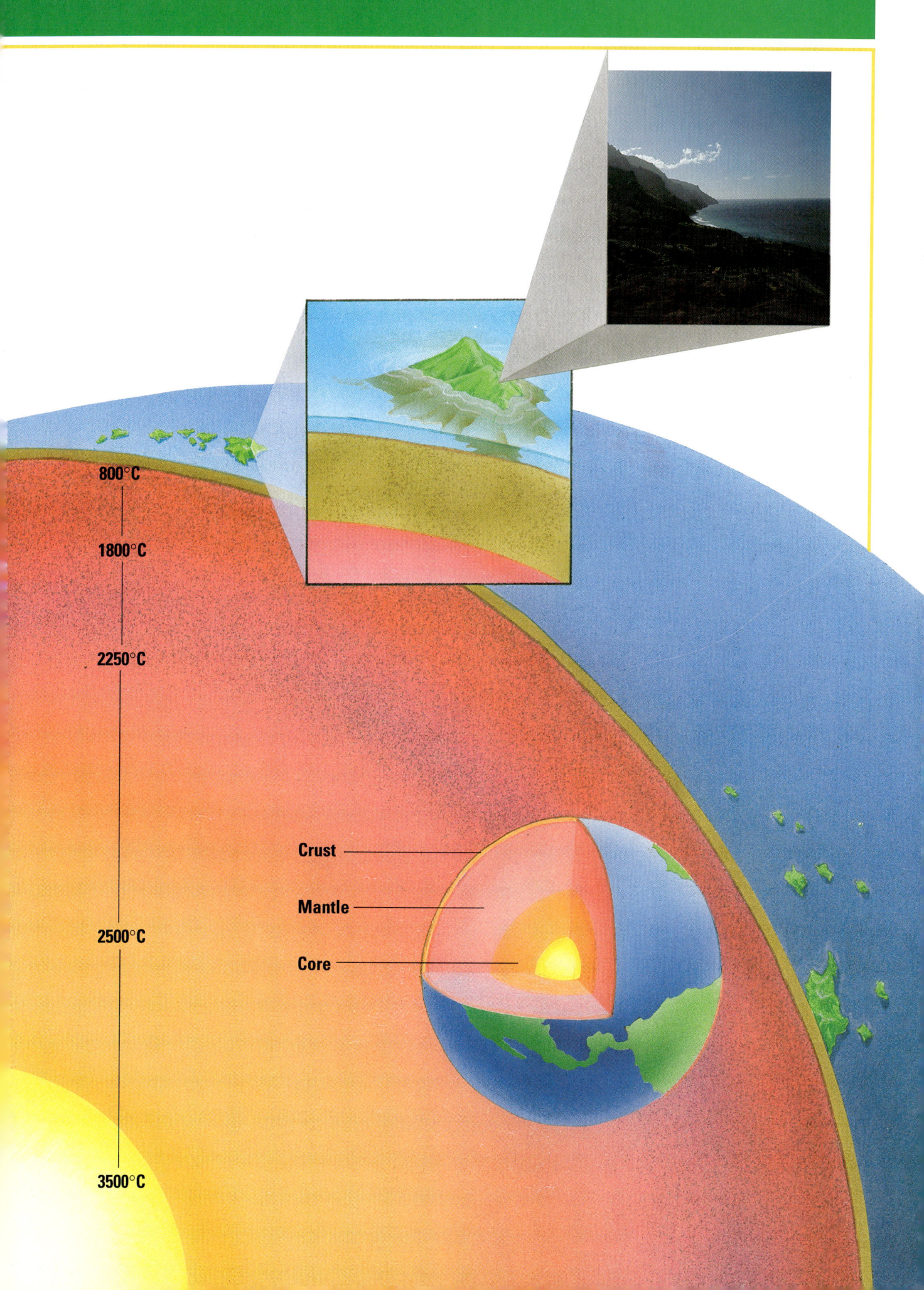

800°C

1800°C

2250°C

2500°C

3500°C

Crust

Mantle

Core

Rising Magma

Magma, which is hot melted rock, also contains gases. The gases within the magma push against the surrounding rock, producing a powerful force. This pushing force is called **pressure.** The pictures below show what happens next.

Magma rises because of its low density. Because of its heat and the high pressure, the magma slowly melts a pathway through the solid rock. When the magma reaches the crust, it forms a large underground lake called a magma chamber. These chambers can be just below the surface of the crust. Magma can gather in the chambers for hundreds of years.

When the magma breaks through the earth's crust, a **volcano** forms. Magma can break through the crust at weak spots. As the pressure in a magma chamber builds, the magma forces its way up through the weak spots, carving a wide channel in the solid rock. The magma then bursts through the crust of the earth, creating a large hole called a central vent.

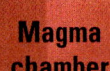

When magma reaches a weak spot in the crust, it forms a magma chamber. Eventually, the magma bursts through the crust, forming a volcano.

Central vent

Hardened lava

Magma chamber

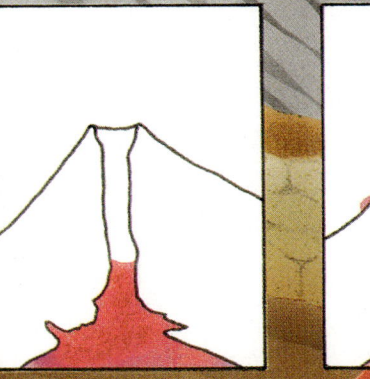
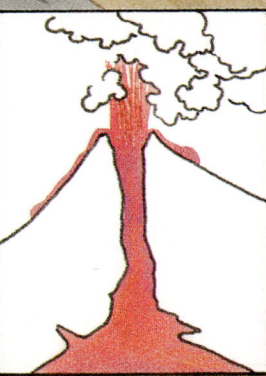

When this type of volcano first erupts, the magma rushes up through the channel. The magma then bursts out of the central vent. The gases in the magma separate from the melted rock and rise high into the air. Now that the magma is on the earth's surface, it is called lava. The lava is still very hot, and it is liquid. The lava pours out onto all sides of the vent. The lava piles up in the shape of a mountain. When the lava stops flowing, it cools and hardens into rock. This volcano may erupt dozens of times in a single year. With each new eruption, the pile of cooled lava grows taller and taller, building up the volcano into a mountain.

Sometimes the central vent of a volcano becomes blocked. In the Kilauea eruptions that began in 1983, the magma burst through a weak spot in the side of the volcano. A new mountain of lava began building up around that vent. Within three years, a new mountain—called Puu Oo—was 250 meters high. Over a half billion cubic meters of lava spilled out of Puu Oo.

Some of the red-hot lava from Puu Oo flowed to the ocean, more than ten kilometers away. As the lava flowed into the cool water, the lava shattered into bits of black rock the size of sand grains. In turn, this sand drifted ashore on the coast of the island of Hawaii. This shattered lava forms Hawaii's famous black-sand beaches.

Checkpoint

1. Draw and label a diagram showing the three main layers of the earth.
2. What makes magma rise through the earth's mantle?
3. **Take Action!** Pour a small amount of cooking oil into a glass of water. Which liquid is like magma? Explain.

MATH

Blow Up

How high can a volcano get? The ash and lava shot out by volcanoes often build up into high mountains. The chart shows the heights of several volcanoes.

Volcano	Height Above Sea Level	
	m	ft
Aconcagua (Argentina)	6959	22,831
Mauna Loa (Hawaii, U.S.A.)	4169	13,677
Mount Fuji (Japan)	3776	12,388
Lassen Peak (California, U.S.A.)	3187	10,457
Paricutin (Mexico)	2808	9213
Mount St. Helens (Washington, U.S.A.)	2549	8364
Mount Katmai (Alaska, U.S.A.)	2047	6715
Vesuvius (Italy)	1277	4190
Surtsey (Iceland)	173	568

What Did You Find Out?
1. *In the chart given, which volcano is the tallest? Which volcano is the shortest?*
2. *When Mount St. Helens erupted in 1980, it lost 396 meters in height. How tall was Mount St. Helens before the eruption?*

1.2 Solid Plates

Are you living on a moving plate?

Your home is the place where you live. It's also the **plate** on which you live. You may not know it, but you've been living on a plate all your life, and so has everybody else who's ever lived on the earth. That's because the earth's crust and the upper part of the mantle is divided into about twenty sections. Each section is called a plate.

These plates fit together like the pieces of a jigsaw puzzle. But unlike jigsaw puzzles you've seen, the picture on this puzzle keeps changing. The picture changes because the plates are always slowly moving. The map on the left shows how the plates move. In some places, the plates are pulling apart. In some places, they are slowly sliding past one another. In other places, the plates are colliding, creating ocean trenches or mountain ranges.

Plates, Pieces of a Puzzle

The plates that cover the earth are between 70 and 150 kilometers thick. Each plate contains a section of the earth's crust and a small part of the upper mantle. The plates float on the upper mantle. Some plates follow the edges of continents. Other plates cut across both land and sea. Together, the plates form the earth's lithosphere, or the layer of rock that lies under the oceans and the air.

▼ Plates are sections of the crust and upper mantle. The arrows show the directions that the plates are moving.

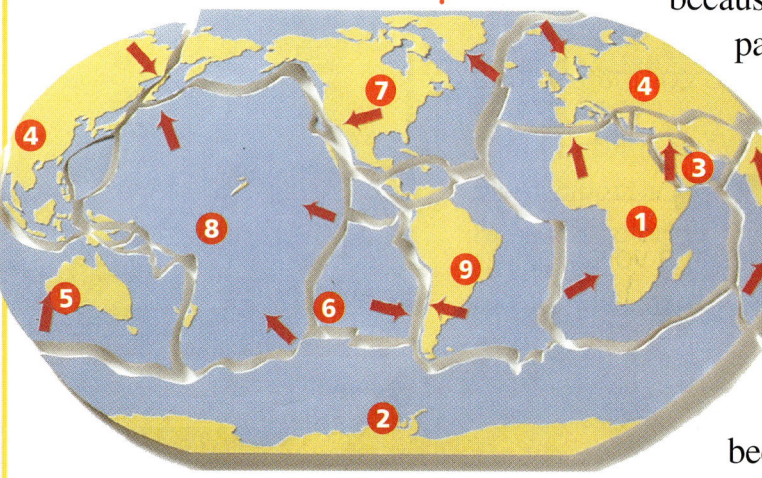

1 African Plate
2 Antarctic Plate
3 Arabian Plate
4 Eurasian Plate
5 Indian Plate
6 Nazca Plate
7 North American Plate
8 Pacific Plate
9 South American Plate

All in a Row

What happens when a hot spot stays put, but the crust above it keeps moving? A chain of islands forms!

Millions of years ago, a hot spot formed under the Pacific Plate. The hot spot melted the mantle and formed magma. The magma rose and formed a volcano. The volcano erupted many times and grew into an island.

Over many years, the Pacific Plate slowly moved away, but the hot spot stayed in the same place. A new volcano formed and grew into an island. As the plate continued moving, new volcanoes formed new islands. Over millions of years, the Hawaiian Islands formed. Today, a new volcano, Loihi, is growing over the hot spot. If it continues to grow, it will become a new Hawaiian Island.

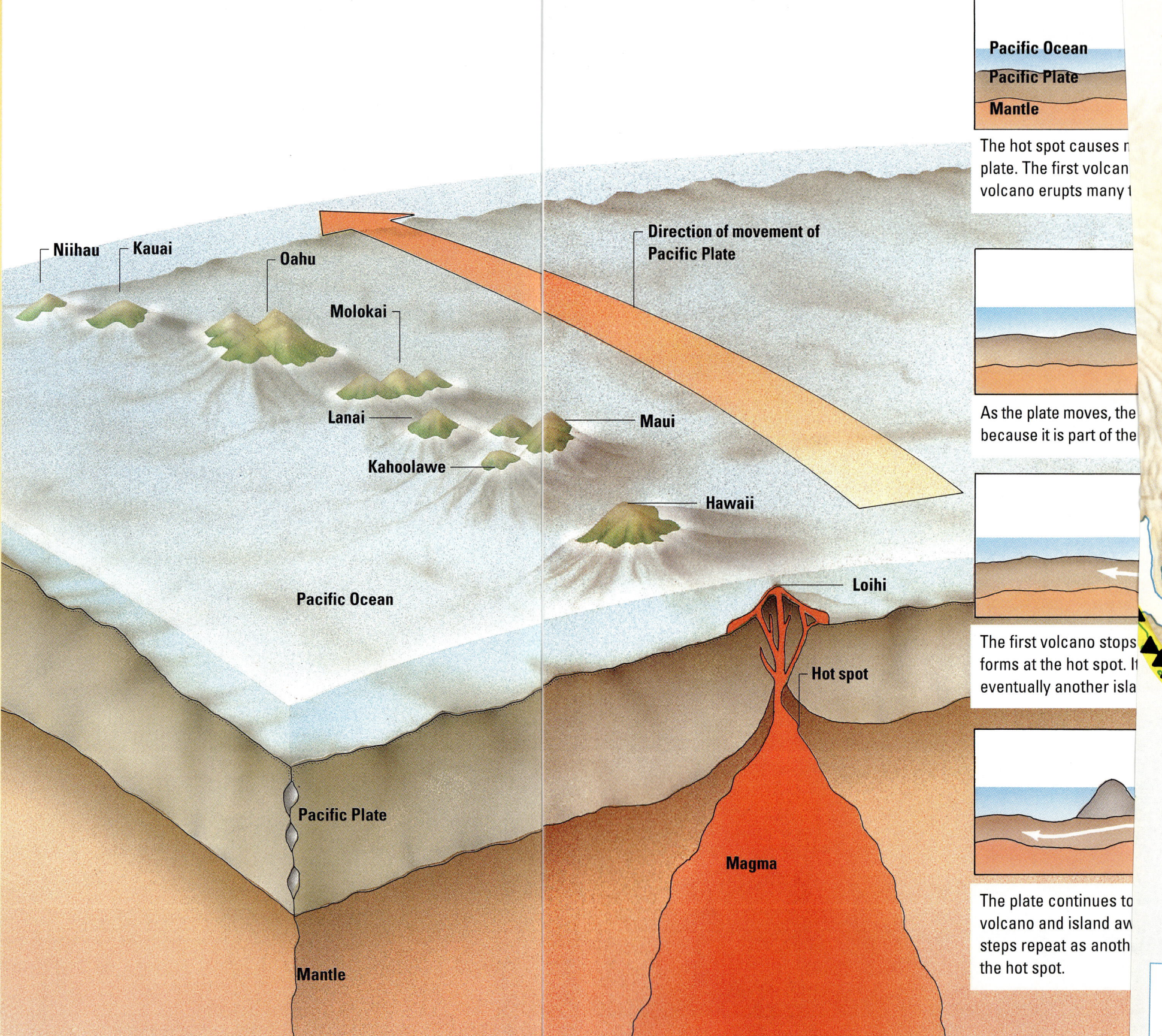

Niihau
Kauai
Oahu
Molokai
Lanai
Maui
Kahoolawe
Hawaii
Loihi

Direction of movement of Pacific Plate

Pacific Ocean

Hot spot

Pacific Plate

Magma

Mantle

Pacific Ocean
Pacific Plate
Mantle

The hot spot causes ... plate. The first volcan... volcano erupts many t...

As the plate moves, the... because it is part of the...

The first volcano stops... forms at the hot spot. It... eventually another isla...

The plate continues to... volcano and island aw... steps repeat as anoth... the hot spot.

Chin

Volca
Ring o

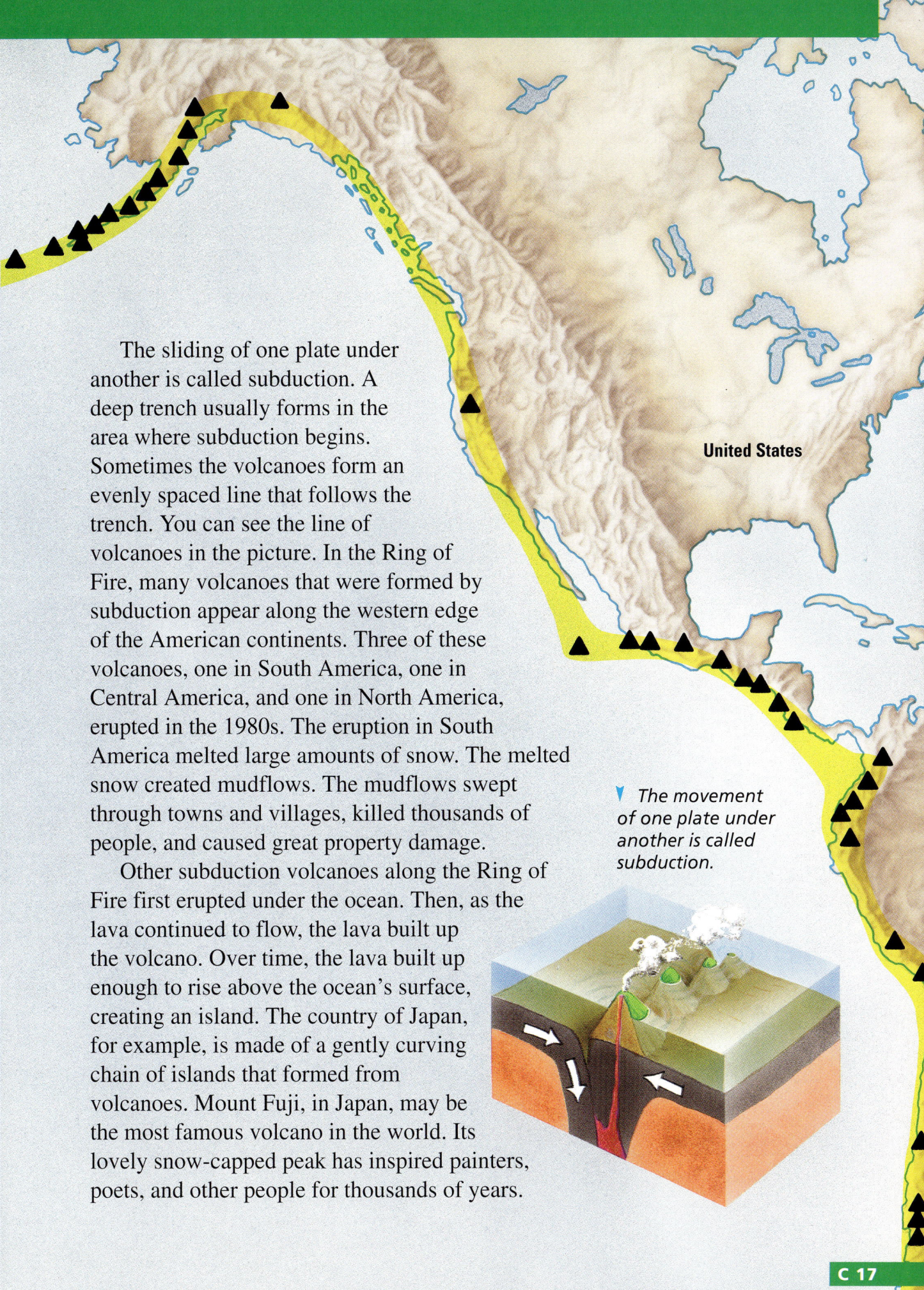

The sliding of one plate under another is called subduction. A deep trench usually forms in the area where subduction begins. Sometimes the volcanoes form an evenly spaced line that follows the trench. You can see the line of volcanoes in the picture. In the Ring of Fire, many volcanoes that were formed by subduction appear along the western edge of the American continents. Three of these volcanoes, one in South America, one in Central America, and one in North America, erupted in the 1980s. The eruption in South America melted large amounts of snow. The melted snow created mudflows. The mudflows swept through towns and villages, killed thousands of people, and caused great property damage.

Other subduction volcanoes along the Ring of Fire first erupted under the ocean. Then, as the lava continued to flow, the lava built up the volcano. Over time, the lava built up enough to rise above the ocean's surface, creating an island. The country of Japan, for example, is made of a gently curving chain of islands that formed from volcanoes. Mount Fuji, in Japan, may be the most famous volcano in the world. Its lovely snow-capped peak has inspired painters, poets, and other people for thousands of years.

United States

The movement of one plate under another is called subduction.

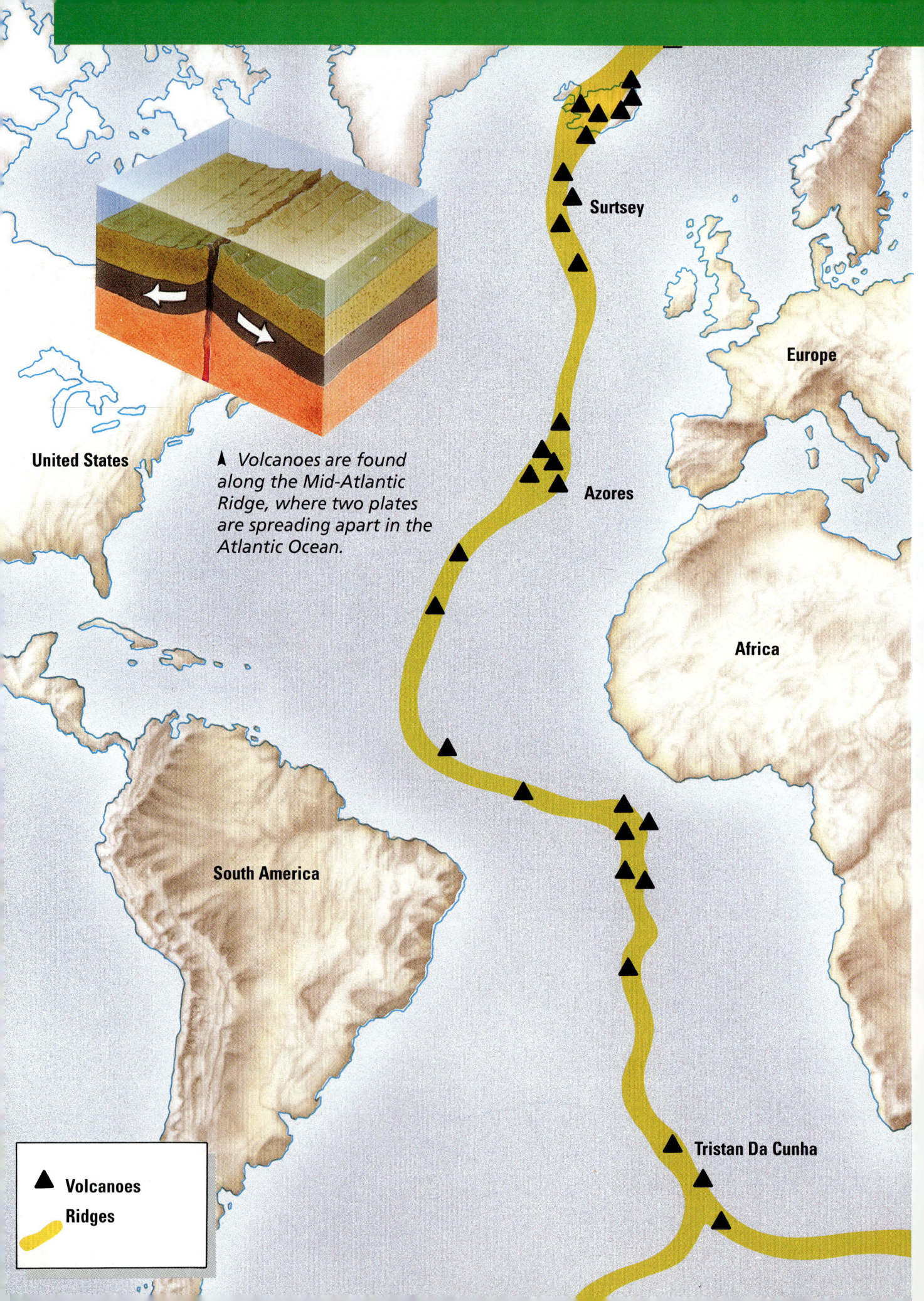

▲ *Volcanoes are found along the Mid-Atlantic Ridge, where two plates are spreading apart in the Atlantic Ocean.*

United States

Europe

Africa

South America

Surtsey

Azores

Tristan Da Cunha

▲ Volcanoes

Ridges

Volcanoes Under the Atlantic

Halfway around the world from the Ring of Fire, another line of volcanoes stretches for thousands of kilometers along the Mid-Atlantic Ridge. But people rarely see the eruptions of these very active volcanoes. Why? Because nearly all of them lie deep beneath the Atlantic Ocean.

The pictures on the left show that the Atlantic Ocean floor is slowly splitting due to movement of the plates under the ocean. One set of plates moves east. The other set moves west. As the plates move apart, magma rises up and erupts under the ocean. The erupting magma forms volcanoes and ridges.

The eruptions of these volcanoes are usually calm and quiet. The great pressure of the ocean water changes the rising magma into harmless chunks of rock called pillow lava. Instead of blasting up into the water, the pillow lava spreads out across the ocean floor. Sometimes, Atlantic volcanoes rise above the ocean's surface and form islands. Surtsey, shown on the right, is an example.

▲ In 1963, Surtsey, an island near Iceland, rose above the ocean. It formed from an underwater Atlantic volcano that had been building up for many years.

Checkpoint

1. Explain what may make plates move.
2. What happens to a volcano when it moves away from a hot spot?
3. What happens to the sliding plate when it slides under another plate?
4. Why are eruptions deep in the ocean calmer than eruptions on land?
5. **Take Action!** Float several pieces of an old puzzle on water in a bowl. Gently stir the water. How do the pieces move? How is this movement like the movement of plates on the earth's surface?

Activity

Egg-citing Earth

When is an egg not an egg? When it is a model of the earth. Use a hard-boiled egg to show the layers of the earth.

Picture A

Picture B

Picture C

Gather These Materials

cover goggles
2 hard-boiled eggs that
  have been soaked in
  vinegar to soften

plastic knife
cutting surface
clear, plastic straw

Follow This Procedure

1 Make a chart like the one on the next page. Record your observations in your chart.

2 Put on your cover goggles.

3 Place a hard-boiled egg that has been soaking in vinegar on a cutting surface. (Picture A)

Predict: *What do you think the inside of the egg will look like?*

4 Firmly hold the egg with one hand. In the other hand hold a knife. Carefully cut the egg in two, shell and all. The egg will be soft after soaking in vinegar. (Picture B) *CAUTION: Handle the knife with care.*

5 In your chart, draw a cross section of the egg. Label it with the 3 parts of the earth that you have learned about.

6 Take the second hard-boiled egg. Push a clear, plastic straw into one end of the shell. (Picture C) Twist the straw to get it into the egg.

Record Your Results

Cross section of egg	Section in the straw

7 Push the straw from one end of the egg all the way out through the other end.

8 What do you see inside the straw? In your chart, draw a picture of the layers of the egg. Label your drawing with the names of the layers of the earth.

State Your Conclusions

1. How many layers can you observe in the first egg? How does the thickness of each layer compare to the other layers?

2. In what ways do the layers of an egg make a good model of the earth?

3. To study the earth's crust, scientists drill into the crust and mantle. Then, they remove long, thin strips of earth. How are the layers in the straw like the layers of the earth?

Let's Experiment

Now that you have used an egg for a model of the earth, how could you make a scale model of the earth using clay?

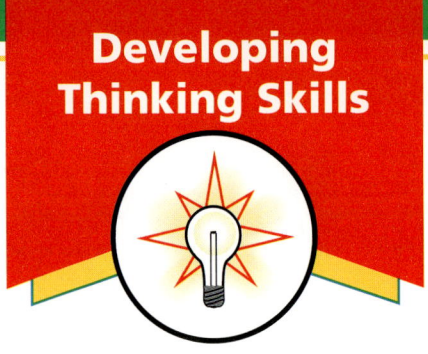

Drawing a Diagram

Did you ever help someone put together a toy from a kit? A diagram probably came with the kit. The diagram showed you how the parts fit together.

Some information is easier to understand if shown in a diagram. A diagram is a good way to show how something works or is put together. Diagrams are often used in everyday life. They are also good study tools. Diagrams can help you remember what you have read.

Thinking It Through

Suppose you were asked to make a diagram of one way that rock is formed from magma. You might draw something like the diagram on this page. Before making a diagram, ask yourself these questions.

1. What do you think the diagram is supposed to show?

2. What parts do I need to label?

3. How can I show how the parts work together? Do I need to draw arrows to show movement from one part to the next? Must I write Step 1, Step 2, Step 3, and so on?

When the diagram is finished, you should ask these questions.

• Is the picture clearly drawn?

• Are all labels clear and easy to understand?

You might show the diagram to someone else to see if he or she understands it.

Your Turn

Use the information you learned in this chapter to make a diagram of how magma moves in the mantle and can form a volcano.

Chapter Review

Thinking Back

1. How is the crust under the ocean different from the continental crust?

2. Describe the earth's core.

3. Where does the **pressure** come from that forces **magma** to rise?

4. How does a **volcano** form?

5. What is the difference between magma and **lava?**

6. Name three ways that **plates** can move in relation to each other.

7. How could convection currents in the mantle cause the plates to move?

8. How does a volcano move away from a hot spot?

9. Describe how the volcanoes along the Ring of Fire formed.

10. How does the movement of the plates in the Atlantic Ocean create volcanoes in the ocean?

Connecting Ideas

1. Copy the concept map. Use the terms to the right to complete the map about how islands and ridges form.

volcanoes   **ridges**
pressure   **islands**

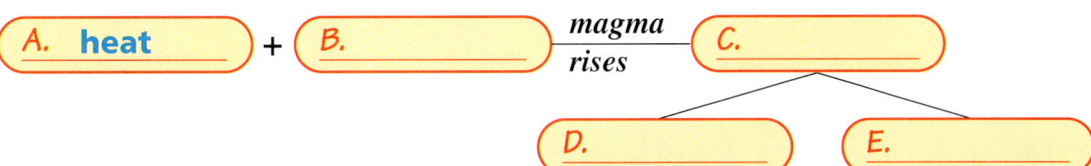

2. Write a sentence or two about the ideas shown in the concept map.

Gathering Evidence

1. In the Activity on page 10, how did the model of the volcano help you understand what a real volcano is like?

2. In the Activity on page 20, how were you able to use the egg as a model of the earth?

Doing Science!

1. *Develop a skit* that would describe how you would have reported the eruption of the Kilauea volcano in 1983 for a news broadcast.

2. *Design an activity* showing the different ways the plates of the earth move.

Explosive Volcanoes

Wear cover goggles
for this activity.

What can pressure do?

Punch a small hole in the lower edge of one side of a shoe box. Insert the neck of a balloon into the hole. The body of the balloon should be inside the box. Cover the balloon with sand or dirt. Predict what will happen when you blow up the balloon. Now blow up the balloon, and see what happens.

For Discussion

1. *What happened when you blew up the balloon?*

2. *How does the amount of air in the balloon affect the result?*

2.1 *Predicting an Eruption*

▶ *Can clouds carry rocks?*

At 8:32 on the morning of May 18, 1980, a huge sheet of rocks begins sliding down the north slope of Mount St. Helens in Washington state. As the rocks slide away, they uncover a gaping crack in the side of the mountain. Within seconds, a boiling hot cloud of rocks, ash, and steam blasts sideways out of the crack. Hugging the ground and moving faster than a race car, the cloud destroys almost everything in its path. It kills more than 60 people and millions of animals and trees. By the time it stops, the cloud has blasted a fan of death across more than 500 square kilometers of land. How can one cloud gather so much power? The answer lurks inside the mountain.

▼ *Before May 18, 1980, Mount St. Helens was covered with forest. The smaller photograph shows rocks, ash, and steam blasting out of the top of Mount St. Helens.*

Warning Signs

Scientists use seismographs to predict the eruption of a volcano. A **seismograph** detects movement, or vibrations, within the earth. The seismograph shows those vibrations by drawing lines on paper. The earth always has some vibration, so the lines are never straight. However, when the vibrations are strong, the seismograph lines begin to move up and down. When there are many strong vibrations, it is more likely that an earthquake will occur, or a volcano will erupt, or both.

Like other volcanoes in the Ring of Fire, Mount St. Helens sits over a magma chamber. When magma begins to rise, it causes earthquakes that can be measured by seismographs. In March of 1980, a seismograph near Mount St. Helens showed that earthquakes were shaking the area. Later that month, a loud explosion ripped open a small crater near the top of the mountain. Then the north side began to bulge outward.

Scientists measured the bulge and found that the bulge was growing, and growing fast. The magma under Mount St. Helens was on the move!

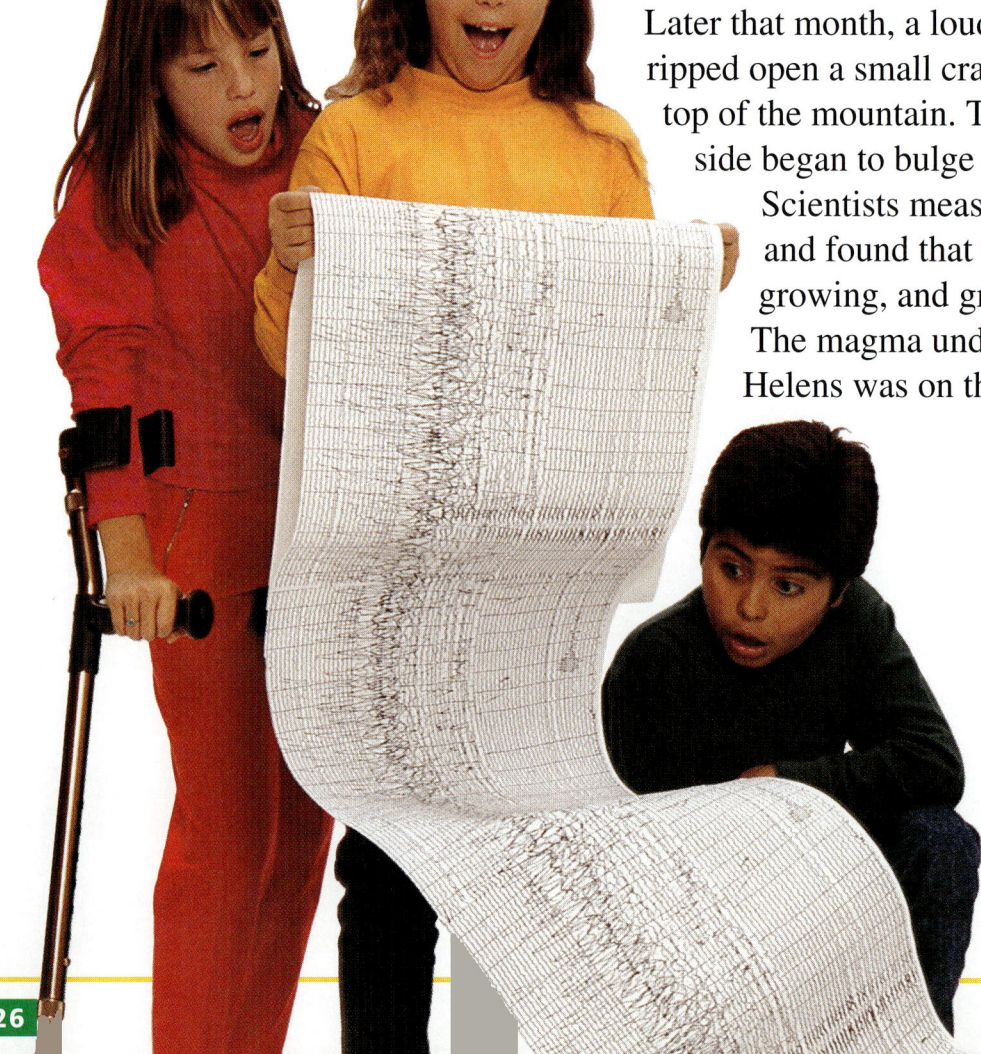

▼ *Students study the record made by a seismograph.*

Bulging Rocks

When you boil water in a pan, the water slowly turns to steam and rises out of the pan. If you put a tight lid on the pan, the steam cannot get out. The pressure in the pan increases. If the pressure gets forceful enough, the pressure can blow the lid off.

Mount St. Helens was like a closed pan of very hot water. Over the years, magma and gases rose inside, and pressure on the crust increased. The magma and gases placed more and more pressure on the mountain's crust, creating the bulge. Then, an earthquake caused the rock atop the mountain to slide downhill. The pressure was suddenly released. The magma and gases rocketed out of the mountain, carrying along a deadly load of ash and rocks.

Because of warnings from many instruments, few people were near Mount St. Helens when it erupted. In 1991, similar instruments warned about the eruption of Mount Pinatubo in the Philippines. Tens of thousands of people left the area.

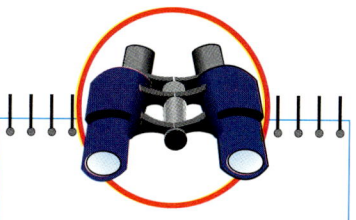

Into The Field

What warning signs can you find?
Volcanoes give warning signs before erupting. Use your senses to observe warning signs that happen before other events.

▲ *Children play with the ash dumped in their neighborhood by the Mount Pinatubo eruption.*

Checkpoint

1. How do scientists use seismographs to help predict an eruption of a volcano?
2. What made Mount St. Helens bulge outward?
3. **Take Action!** Pop off the cap of a bottle of warm soda. Explain how the soda is like the magma at Mount St. Helens.

Activity

Up from the Ashes

A volcano spreads black volcanic ash over the land. Can plants survive being covered by volcanic ash? Try this activity to find out.

Picture A

Picture B

Picture C

Gather These Materials

2 paper cups
soil
12 small fast-growing
  seeds such as beans
scissors

sheet of black
  construction paper
beaker
water

Follow This Procedure

1 Make a chart like the one on the next page. Record your observations in your chart.

2 Fill 2 paper cups with the same amount of soil.

3 Plant 6 identical seeds in each cup. (Picture A)

4 Use scissors to cut a sheet of black construction paper into tiny pieces. (Picture B) The black pieces will represent the black volcanic ash left after a volcano erupts.

5 Take one cup. Cover its soil with a layer of black paper pieces. The layer should be about 3 mm thick. (Picture C)

6 Water the 2 cups with the same amount of water. Put both cups in the same place.

Predict: In which of the cups will the seeds grow first?

Record Your Results

Observations		
Date	Cup without "ash"	Cup with "ash"

7 Record your observations. Record when you first see the sprouts, how many seeds grow in each cup, and how tall each plant grows.

State Your Conclusions

1. In which cup did you see sprouts first? Why?

2. How does this activity help explain what occurs to an area after a volcano erupts?

3. What did the seedlings under the black paper bits look like? Why?

Let's Experiment

You have now seen how a layer of ash affects the growth of seeds. Do an experiment to show whether the thickness of the ash makes a difference in how the seeds grow.

Recovering from Eruptions

▶ *Is there life after an eruption?*

In the photograph below, firs, hemlocks, and other evergreen trees ring the calm waters of Spirit Lake, not far from Mount St. Helens. The photograph was taken before May 18, 1980. On that fateful May date, a deadly cloud of ash and rocks from the erupting volcano swept across Spirit Lake. The cloud knocked down trees and left behind a thick, heavy carpet of gray and gritty ash, as shown in the photograph at the bottom of the next page.

Would the land around Spirit Lake ever recover? The trees were dead, and the waters of the lake were thick with mud. Yet underneath that barren landscape, life stirred within hours of the eruption. Chipmunks scurried along their underground tunnels. Frogs underwater were still alive. They showed that Spirit Lake had a chance.

▼ *Spirit Lake, before the eruption of Mount St. Helens*

Underground Survivors

When plants or animals live through a disaster in a particular area, they are called survivors. Many plants and animals survived the eruption.

Chipmunks and pocket gophers live underground. When the ash and rocks fell around Mount St. Helens, many of them were safe beneath the soil. Over time, they dug their way up through the ash and poked their heads above ground. If they lived near water, they might have seen a few frogs, salamanders, crayfish, or snakes. Mud, water, and ice had protected these water animals.

But what about the plants? In between the fallen trees, a hardy plant called fireweed began growing within a month of the eruption. Fireweed gets its name because it grows soon after forest fires. It can grow after eruptions as well. All across Mount St. Helens, clumps of fireweed sprang out of the ground and bloomed with beautiful pink flowers. Other plants also grew, such as huckleberry. The plants attracted hungry animals from far away. These animals came from areas that the eruption had not damaged, so they cannot be called survivors.

▲ Roots and bulbs buried under the soil survived the eruption of Mount St. Helens.

▼ Spirit Lake, after the eruption of Mount St. Helens

Distant Colonizers

Colonizers are living things that come into an area to eat and live. After the eruption in May, deer and elk were among the first colonizers to enter the ash-covered land around Mount St. Helens. The deer and elk came to eat the fireweed and the other plants. As they picked their way across the land, they left deep hoof prints in the ash. They also left animal wastes filled with seeds. Over time, the seeds from the animal wastes sprouted and began to grow into plants. These seeds and plants were also colonizers because they came from outside the ash-covered land.

Rainfall and melting snow carved channels where plants could grow. Gophers broke through the ash from underground and shoved out small mounds of dirt. Seeds blown by the wind landed in these mounds and channels. Some of the seeds were from willow and cottonwood trees. Others came from blooming flowers. These seeds also sprouted and began to grow.

As the plants grew during the summer of 1980, they attracted more and more animals. Insects and spiders began to arrive. And wherever insects go, birds are sure to follow. Birds came to eat the insects and to build nests.

The dead trees were home to many living things. Inside the trees, bacteria and fungi ate the wood, turning it into rotten matter that enriched the ground. Around the trees, a few saplings rose from the old roots and stretched their leaves toward the sun and the rain.

By autumn, many forms of life could be found in the area around Mount St. Helens. Some were survivors and others were colonizers, but all showed that life would go on. Someday soon, Spirit Lake and all the other places near the volcano would once again be green and growing.

◄ Lupine, a plant with lovely colorful flowers, grew through the ash of the Mount St. Helens eruption.

The Healing of Mount St. Helens

Plants are key to the return of life.

On May 18, 1980, Mount St. Helens violently erupted. Only a few living things survived. The fireweed plant was the first to start growing. Deer, elk, and birds came through the area soon after the eruption. They did not stay because there was little food or shelter.

When the fireweed plants died, they fell into the ash and made the soil richer. The wind blew in new seeds. Many different plants started growing. The plants attracted insects, birds, and other animals. By 1990, the trees and shrubs were large enough to provide shelter, and there was enough food. Deer, elk, and birds once again were living on Mount St. Helens.

1980 Soon after the eruption, fireweed starts growing through the ash.

1983 Several years after the eruption, the soil has gotten richer. More kinds of plants are growing.

1980	1982

1986 Trees are the last plants to return. Here, Douglas fir trees have started growing, but they are still small.

1990 Many kinds of living things have returned. But the land is not yet the same as it was before the eruption.

1984   1986   1988   1990

► *Beautiful flowers also grow in volcanic soil.*

▼ *Ash from volcanoes makes the soil in Indonesia very fertile. Indonesia is a leading producer of rice.*

Benefits From Below

Volcanoes can kill people and reshape land, but they also provide many life-giving substances. Much of the air we breathe and the water we drink came from volcanoes. Without eruptions, many important gases would remain deep within the earth.

Volcanoes also help build the land on which we live by forming islands. Hawaii, Japan, and many other islands are volcanoes, although some of them are no longer active. But those are just the volcanoes that reach the surface of the ocean. Lava flows from volcanoes cover the deep ocean floor.

Another type of rock—granite—lies under the continents. Granite forms from magma that cools beneath the ground without erupting. Granite is very hard. People use granite to construct buildings that last for centuries.

The magma that erupts as lava contains many useful minerals. Obsidian is a shiny black volcanic glass that Native Americans used for making knives, arrowheads, and jewelry. Pumice, on the other hand, is a light, white, foamy-looking rock that when ground into a powder is used for polishing and scrubbing.

The ash that erupts from some volcanoes begins to break down soon after falling to the ground. Over time, it gives the soil nutrients important for plant growth. In the rich volcanic soil of Indonesia, for example, farmers grow rice, corn, peanuts, coffee, and many other crops. Volcanoes loom above the farmers' fertile fields, ready to erupt at any moment.

Italy's Mount Vesuvius has erupted several times in the past few hundred years, but farmers have always returned to its fertile slopes. There they grow apricots, grapes, tomatoes, beans, peas, and millions of beautiful carnations that are shipped all over Europe. Volcanoes may be dangerous, but for these farmers, volcanoes are well worth the risk.

Somewhat less risky are the underground steam fields that are found near volcanoes. People have begun using this underground steam to make electricity. At the Geysers power plant, located near volcanoes in northern California, the steam rises up to the plant through large pipes. The powerful steam drives huge turbines inside the plant. These turbines create enough electricity to serve one million people. That's a lot of electricity, but it's just a tiny fraction of the incredible power that is within volcanoes.

Checkpoint

1. What's the difference between survivors and colonizers?
2. How did deer and elk help life return to Mount St. Helens?
3. In 1981, the elk did not stay in the area around Mount St. Helens. Why?
4. In what ways do volcanoes contribute to life on the earth?
5. **Take Action!** Make a list of uses of the underground steam fields found near volcanoes.

Traveling Seeds

 Wear cover goggles for this activity.

Does the shape of a seed help it travel?

What To Do
A. Cut three squares, 5 centimeters on each side, out of paper.
B. Roll one square into a ball. Fold one square in half. Pretend that each piece is a seed.
C. Turn a fan on low speed. Drop each "seed" in front of the fan.
D. Measure how far away each "seed" landed from where you dropped it. Record your answers on a table like the one below.
E. Use the third square to invent a "seed" that will travel far. Test it with the fan.

Record Your Data

	Seed Number		
	1	2	3
Distance traveled			

What Did You Find Out?
1. *Which "seed" traveled farthest?*
2. *How did its shape help it travel far?*
3. *Which "seed" might travel on the wind to a volcano? Which might not? Why?*

Activity

Bulbs or Seeds?

Flowers such as tulips, crocuses, and daffodils grow from bulbs, not seeds. How are bulbs different from seeds? Do this activity to find out.

Picture A

Picture B

Gather These Materials

cover goggles

bulbs such as tulip, crocus, or daffodil

seeds

paper towel

plastic knife

iodine solution

cups and flowerpots with soil

water

hand lens

Follow This Procedure

1. Make charts like the ones on the next page. Record your observations in your charts.

2. Put on your cover goggles.

3. Examine a bulb and a seed carefully. (Picture A) Write your observations on your chart.

4. Place a bulb on a paper towel. Carefully use the knife to cut off a small piece of the bulb. *CAUTION: Use the knife with care.*

5. Get the iodine. Iodine turns blue-black when it is put on something that has starch in it. Starch is a form of food found in plants. *CAUTION: Handle iodine with care. It is a chemical that can stain hands and clothes. Clean up spills and wash up immediately.*

Predict: Will the iodine turn blue-black when you put it on a piece of bulb?

Picture C

Record Your Results

	Bulb	Seed
Name		
Description		
Iodine test		
Depth of planting		

Observations of growth

Date	Bulb	Seed

6 Place a few drops of iodine solution on the piece of bulb. (Picture B) What happens to the iodine? Record your results in your chart.

7 Try the iodine test on some seeds and record your results in the chart.

8 Plant several bulbs and seeds in the soil, following your teacher's directions or the package instructions. (Picture C) Record the depth of planting for each. Water the bulbs and seeds.

9 Observe your plants for several weeks. Record your observations.

State Your Conclusions

1. Do bulbs or seeds have more stored food for the young plant?

2. Which group is planted at a greater depth within the soil?

3. Which group would have a better chance of surviving after a volcano erupts? Why?

Let's Experiment

You have seen that bulbs and seeds store different amounts of starch and that they should be planted at different depths. Now find out if seeds and bulbs can grow at different temperatures.

Hypothesizing

One of the main volcanoes on the island of Hawaii is Kilauea (Kē′lou ā′ə). For more than seven years, streams of burning lava have flowed down its slopes. This lava has cooled into a hard, dark mass. You might think that nothing could grow here. But the Hawaiian Islands were formed by volcanoes that were built up from lava, and they are full of plant and animal life. Scientists used these and other facts to form the hypothesis that life would return to Kilauea.

A hypothesis is an explanation that scientists think is correct because it is based on known facts. A hypothesis is not a fact itself.

Thinking It Through

You are a scientist who is studying the return of living organisms to Kilauea. You observed the lava slopes, and learned the following facts:

Fact 1: Tiny plants called mosses are growing on the cooled lava.

Fact 2: The 'ohi'a trees on Kilauea were badly burned during the eruption. But some have an unburned side. The unburned sides of the 'ohi'a trees are growing new buds. These buds are growing little roots into the air. The roots get water from fog and rain.

Fact 3: Silversword plants are blooming on the volcano's crater. Bees, snails, wasps, beetles, and spiders have arrived.

Using what you observed, your hypothesis is that the cooled lava on Kilauea will be able to support further life. To test this hypothesis, you could see how many more living things arrive over time.

Your Turn

Use the facts in the chapter to form a hypothesis about why an island is forming at Spot A, a place where two oceanic plates are moving apart. List the facts that you used to form your hypothesis.

Chapter Review

Thinking Back

1. What tool do scientists use to predict the eruption of a volcano?
2. What does a **seismograph** detect?
3. How can seismographs save lives?
4. How do some small animals survive volcanic eruptions?
5. Why do animals come to areas where a volcano has erupted?
6. How do seeds get to an area where a volcano has erupted?

7. How did plants help animals return to Mount St. Helens after the eruption?
8. How do volcanic eruptions help produce air and water?
9. What useful rocks are formed by magma and lava?
10. Why do farmers return to the slopes of volcanoes?

Connecting Ideas

1. Copy the concept map. Use the terms to the right to complete the map about the benefits from volcanoes.

air and water   ash
gases   rich soil
useful rocks

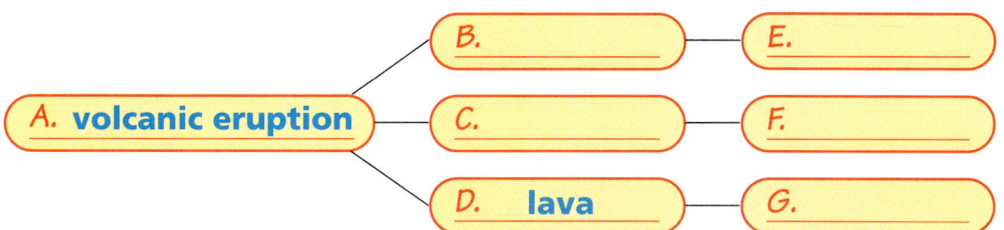

A. volcanic eruption
B. _____
C. _____
D. lava
E. _____
F. _____
G. _____

2. Write a sentence or two about the ideas shown in the concept map.

Gathering Evidence

1. In the Activity on page 28, what evidence did you use to decide whether ash is good or bad for plants?
2. In the Activity on page 38, which might better survive a volcanic eruption, a seed or a bulb? Why?

Doing Science!

1. **Design a display** that shows both the harmful and positive results of volcanic eruptions.
2. **Write a news broadcast** describing how an area recovered from the eruption of a volcano.

CHAPTER

3

Faults and Quakes

> Push and presto! It's an instant mountain.

Discover Activity

How do mountains form?

Flatten out three pieces of clay into rectangles. Place them on top of one another. Then put a block at each narrow end of the stack of clay. Press the two blocks toward each other. What happens?

For Discussion

1. Does it make a difference whether you press hard or soft against the blocks? What is the difference?

2. What do the blocks and the clay stand for?

Raising the Ground

▶ **Are all mountains volcanoes?**

Far to the south of Mount St. Helens, the rocky eastern side of Mount Whitney rises steeply out of the California desert. The jagged peak of the mountain soars more than 4000 meters above sea level. The peak is just one part of a long line of tall, jagged mountains that begins near Mount Whitney and stretches north for more than 600 kilometers along the eastern edge of California, as you can see in the picture. From a distance, the line of mountains looks like the blade of a giant saw covered with snow. For this reason, the Spanish settlers called them the Sierra Nevada—the snow-clad saw.

Did the Sierra Nevada erupt out of the ground like a volcano? Probably not. All along the eastern edge of the Sierras runs a fault. A **fault** is a crack in the earth's crust and upper mantle along which rock moves. The eastern side of the Sierras is slowly rising up along this fault in big blocks. Because the Sierra Nevada mountains are moving up in big blocks along a fault, they are called fault-block mountains. Their eastern side is steep, but their western side rolls gently down to California's central valley.

Fault-block mountains are just one of several types of mountains that cover the face of the earth. In this lesson, you will learn more about fault-block mountains and folded mountains. Both types can be found in the United States.

▼ *On this map of the western United States, you can see the Sierra Nevada near the eastern border of California.*

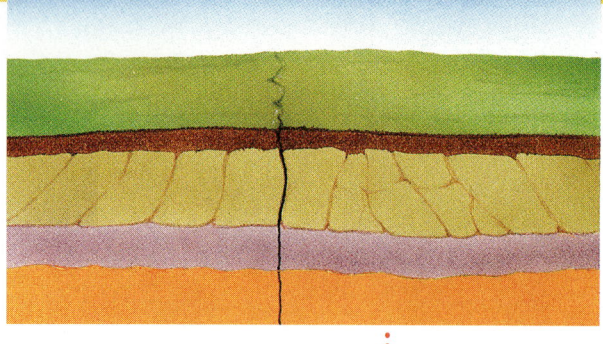

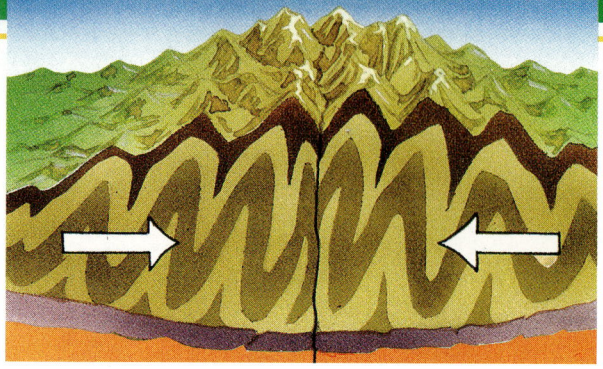

▲ *Folded mountains, like the Appalachians, form when two plates collide and crumple up.*

▼ *Appalachian Mountains*

Folded Mountains

To understand folded mountains, you have to remember that the earth is covered with slowly moving plates made of layers of rock. Folded mountains form when two plates collide. The force of the collision slowly crumples the edges of the plates, forming mountains. This mountain-building process can continue for millions of years, as the edges of the plates continue to crumple. The drawing above shows what the folded layers of rock under these mountains are like.

About 400 million years ago, the African Plate began smashing into the eastern edge of the North American Plate, forming the Appalachian Mountains. Over millions of years, the Appalachians slowly rose thousands of meters into the air. Then rainfall and wind wore down the Appalachians. The softer rocks washed away, leaving gently rounded mountains.

Today, the Appalachians are less than half as tall as the Sierras. Instead of being a single line of jagged peaks like the Sierras, the Appalachians are a series of ridges separated by valleys. These ridges and valleys follow the folds of the rock layers below the surface. If you stand on top of a ridge, you can see the other ridges stretching away from you like the crests of gentle waves. Judging from the view, you would never know that the Appalachians probably were once the tallest mountains on earth.

Fault-Block Mountains

The Sierras are much younger than the Appalachians. The Sierras began to form about 100–150 million years ago, when a plate separating from the Pacific Plate started sliding under the western edge of the North American Plate. As the Pacific Plate slid beneath the North American Plate and deep into the mantle, some of its rocks melted into magma. Instead of rising to the surface through volcanoes, some of the magma cooled underground and became granite. As more and more granite built up along the Sierra line, the granite began pushing upward in huge blocks.

As the granite blocks rose, they made cracks in the crust. One of these cracks is now the long fault that runs all along the eastern edge of the Sierras.

When the granite blocks move up along this fault, they create earthquakes. The east side of the Sierras has had many earthquakes in recent years. Based on these recent earthquakes and other available evidence, scientists think that the Sierras are still rising.

▲ *Fault-block mountains, like the Sierras, form when a block of rock moves up along a fault.*

Checkpoint

1. How do folded mountains form?
2. Why are the Sierras called fault-block mountains?
3. **Take Action!** Build your own mountain, then tell where your mountain is and how it formed.

Activity

Something Has to Give

What happens when two of the earth's plates collide with each other? Try this activity to find out.

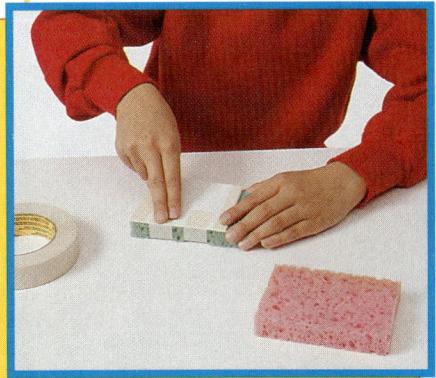

Picture A

Picture B

Picture C

Gather These Materials

cover goggles
scissors
4 index cards
masking tape

4 dry sponges
2 desks
rubber bands

Follow This Procedure

1 Make a chart like the one on the next page. Record your observations in your chart.

2 Put on your cover goggles.

3 Use scissors to cut four index cards in half. Make a pile of the eight pieces, and tape the stack together.

4 Place the cards on one edge of a dry sponge. Attach them with masking tape. (Picture A)

5 Use two desks that are the same height. Move them close together so there is a distance of one "sponge length" between them.

6 Place the sponge with the index cards on one desk. Place a plain sponge of the same type on the other desk.

Predict: *What do you think will happen when the two sponges collide?*

7 Slowly push the two sponges toward each other, as shown in Picture B. Record your observations.

8 Place a sponge on top of each of the original sponges. These second sponges will represent a continent on a moving plate.

9 Attach the top and bottom sponges together with rubber bands so that the top sponges are curved with the ends upward. (Picture C)

10 Move the sponges toward each other until the continents collide. Record your observations.

Record Your Results

Observations	
Single sponges	
Double sponges	

State Your Conclusions

1. What happens when 2 of the earth's plates collide? What do you think happens to the lower plate?
2. How does this activity help to explain how mountains are formed along the borders of the earth's plates?

Let's Experiment

The ocean floor is made of dense rock and is also riding on a plate. Make a model to show what happens when a plate carrying the ocean floor collides with a plate carrying land.

3.2 *Shaking the Land*

Can the earth stop the World Series?

On October 17, 1989, baseball fans from all around San Francisco came to Candlestick Park for the third game of the World Series. At five in the afternoon, the crowd watched the players get ready for the first pitch. At that moment, about 40 kilometers south of Candlestick Park, part of the Pacific Plate near Loma Prieta suddenly moved northward and upward. A few seconds later, the baseball park and almost everything else in the Bay Area began to shake. Roads collapsed. Many houses collapsed, as shown in the picture. Fires broke out. Although the shaking lasted only 15 seconds, there was much damage. Back at Candlestick Park, the fans were terrified, but luckily no one was killed. The World Series was postponed. The Loma Prieta earthquake had just shaken the Bay Area, and normal life had come to a halt.

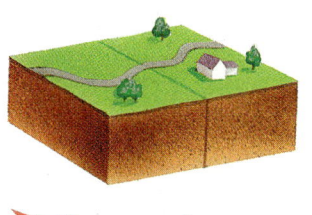

▲ *The top picture shows a fault before an earthquake. The bottom picture shows how the blocks of crust moved during the earthquake.*

▼ *These houses in San Francisco collapsed during the earthquake of October 17, 1989.*

Sliding Along

Earthquakes begin at faults. Many faults occur where two plates meet. For example, the Loma Prieta earthquake began along the San Andreas Fault. This fault, which is 1200 kilometers long, is one of the places where the North American and Pacific Plates meet.

The Pacific Plate is slowly moving to the northwest. As this plate moves, it slides past the North American Plate. Both plates are made of layers of rocks. In some places, the rocks slide past each other easily. In other places, the rocks stick. These sticking places are usually several kilometers below the earth's surface. Pressure builds in the sticking places until the rocks break. Then the Pacific Plate suddenly lurches northward, starting an earthquake. The San Andreas Fault is one place where pressure often builds up and earthquakes occur.

Into The Field

Are you prepared for a natural emergency? *Think of all the things you would need in case of a natural emergency in your area. Make a list and prepare a box of those things.*

▼ The San Francisco earth-quake in 1906 was more powerful than the Loma Prieta earthquake. In 1906, most of the buildings, like the one in the small picture, were destroyed.

Super-House

Special features in houses can help protect them during an earthquake.

Houses are damaged during earthquakes because the earth shakes back and forth. As a result, the house shakes back and forth. Imagine standing in your home. Imagine that an earthquake is shaking your house or apartment back and forth. What do you think might happen? The house might shake off its foundation (the part under the house that the house sits on). The roof might fall off, or the chimney might break. Pipes that carry water or gas might break. Furniture could fall over. Dishes, books, and other things could fall out of cabinets. Windows might break. The picture shows a house that has been built to be safe during an earthquake.

Safety film is put on the windows. The film sticks to glass and holds it together if the glass breaks.

Special bolts are used to connect the floor of the house to the foundation. Similar bolts are used to hold the roof to the walls of the house.

Pieces of metal are used to hold the water heater in place.

Pieces of metal are used to hold the chimney in place so that it won't fall off the roof.

Pieces of metal called brackets are used to attach bookcases and cabinets to the walls so that the bookcases and cabinets won't fall over.

Pieces of metal are used to hold gas and water pipes to the walls.

Hooks on refrigerator and cabinet doors keep the things inside from falling out.

▲ LANDSAT, a satellite, took this picture. It shows the San Andreas Fault in the Monterey Bay area just south of San Francisco.

▼ These students are putting together an earthquake emergency kit.

Being Prepared

You can see where part of the San Andreas Fault is located in the photograph on the left. Scientists know that earthquakes are likely to occur along these faults, but they don't know exactly when. They can only make rough guesses based on past earthquakes and present warning signs.

In order to gather information about possible earthquakes, scientists use seismographs, tiltmeters, and laser reflectors—the same tools that can help them predict the eruptions of volcanoes.

When predicting earthquakes along a fault, scientists also consider how much time has passed since the last major earthquake. Along the San Andreas Fault, for example, earthquakes that measure 6 or more on the Richter scale occur about every 100 years. This information helps scientists predict when the next earthquake might occur.

But past history is not enough. Scientists also watch for warning signs. Sometimes small quakes occur just before a bigger quake. Sometimes animals behave in strange ways. But these warning signs don't always occur. Scientists have yet to find a warning that occurs before every earthquake.

Earthquakes can be very dangerous. If you live in an area that might have an earthquake, your best protection is to be prepared.

You should keep an earthquake kit in your home. The kit should include flashlights, batteries, a fire extinguisher, a portable radio, a first-aid kit, water, warm clothes, and canned food.

If you are inside during an earthquake, go under a table and cover your head. The table will protect you from falling objects. If you are in a car, tell the driver to pull over to the side of the road. Stay inside the car and keep away from bridges, power lines, and large buildings.

Checkpoint

1. What happens when sliding plates stick together?
2. What could you do to make your home safer during an earthquake?
3. What warning signs may show that an earthquake is about to occur?
4. Take Action! For a month, look in newspapers for reports of earthquakes. Record when and where the earthquakes occur.

Richter Scale

The Richter scale compares the strength of earthquakes. Each increase of one stands for an earthquake that is ten times as strong. For example, an earthquake of 6 is ten times as strong as an earthquake of 5.

Richter Number	Damage Caused
2.0–2.9	Not felt, but recorded
3.0–3.9	Felt by a few people
4.0–4.9	Felt by most people
5.0–5.9	Slight damage to buildings
6.0–6.9	Much damage to buildings
7.0–7.9	Great damage to buildings
8.0–8.9	Total destruction

What Did You Find Out?
1. *The Loma Prieta earthquake measured 7.1 on the Richter scale. The San Francisco earthquake of 1906 measured 8.3. Which was stronger?*
2. *Every day more than 1000 earthquakes occur, but no one feels them. What do these earthquakes measure on the Richter scale?*

Activity

Shake and Quake

Does the shape of a building help it remain standing during an earthquake? Try this activity to find out.

Picture A

Picture B

Picture C

Gather These Materials

shoe-box lid

metric ruler

2 books of the same size

30 sugar cubes

Follow This Procedure

1 Make a chart like the one on the next page. Record your observations in your chart.

2 In the center of a shoe-box lid, draw a square 12 cm long on each side. (Picture A)

3 Balance the shoe-box lid on 2 books.

4 Use sugar cubes to build a different "building" in each corner. Each building should have a different design and number. (Picture B)

Predict: *Which of your buildings will be the least likely to fall during an earthquake?*

5 Use your fingers in a flicking motion to strike under the center of the lid. (Picture C) Record your observations.

6 Strike the lid again, using slightly more force than before. Which buildings are still standing?

7 Repeat several more times, increasing the force each time until all the buildings have fallen. Record your results.

Record Your Results

Number of building	Strength of force needed (from 1 to 10 with 1 being the weakest) to make building fall
1	
2	
3	
4	
Your own design	

8 In one corner of the square, construct a building using at least 6 sugar cubes. Can you make it earthquake proof? Build it and shake it to see.

State Your Conclusions

1. Which building fell first? Why?

2. How did you use your shake and quake results to design your own building?

3. What would you recommend to someone who wanted to build a house in an area that has earthquakes?

Let's Experiment

Repeat your experiment. But this time, make a scale that shows how strong your earthquakes are.

Analyzing Information

When you need to solve a problem, you can analyze the information you have. When you analyze information, you study it carefully. Some ways to analyze information include finding time and space relationships and using diagrams.

Thinking It Through

Suppose you were asked to analyze the layers of sedimentary rock shown in the diagram at the right. You could begin by studying how the layers are related in time and space. You could then use this information to draw your conclusions about the history of the area. To draw your conclusions, you might ask questions like these.

What do I know about the way layers of rock are related?

I know that the oldest layers are usually on the bottom. Therefore, the location of the layers (space) is connected to when the layers were deposited (time).

How can I use this information to determine the age of any fossils that I might find?

Since the fossils are in the rock, they must have been deposited with the rock. Analyzing this information, I can conclude the older the layer of rock, the older the fossil.

Can I find out more about the history of this place from these layers?

Yes, I can. After looking at the diagram and analyzing the information it shows, I think the shell fossil layer might mean that at one time a sea was in this area.

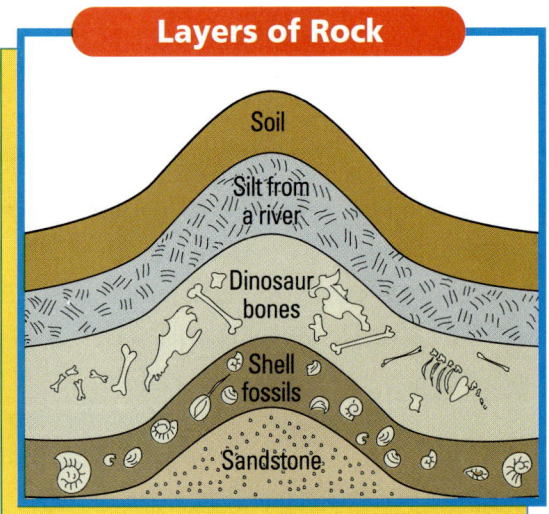

Layers of Rock

Soil

Silt from a river

Dinosaur bones

Shell fossils

Sandstone

Your Turn

Analyze the diagram to answer the following questions.

1. Do you think this area was ever covered by a river?

2. Did dinosaurs live in this area before or after it was a sea?

3. What do you think the fold in the layers might mean?

Chapter Review

Thinking Back

1. What is a **fault**?

2. What kind of mountains are the Appalachians and how did they form?

3. Why are the Appalachians no longer the tallest mountains in the world?

4. What kind of mountains are the Sierras and how did they form?

5. Why do earthquakes occur where two plates meet?

6. If you had a house in an area that has earthquakes, what would you do to your house to make it safer?

7. Can scientists predict exactly when an earthquake will occur? Why or why not?

8. Name some tools that scientists use to study earthquakes.

9. What goes into an earthquake kit?

10. What should you do if you are in a building or in a car during an earthquake?

Connecting Ideas

1. Copy the concept map. Use the terms to the right to complete the map about the formation of mountains.

fault-block   **folded**

Appalachians

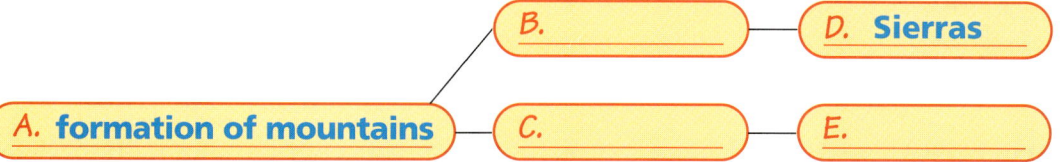

2. Write a sentence or two about the ideas shown in the concept map.

Gathering Evidence

1. In the Activity on page 46, how did the sponges show what happens to continental plates when they collide?

2. In the Activity on page 54, how could you predict which buildings were least likely to fall?

Doing Science!

1. **Design a model** to show the different ways mountains are formed.

2. **Develop a plan** for a person who lives in an area that has earthquakes. How could that person inform neighbors about ways to be prepared for an earthquake?

Earthquake-proof Buildings?

Earthquakes occur often in certain areas. Earthquakes can't be prevented, and so far they can't be predicted. However, if buildings are built in a special way, they are less likely to shake apart during an earthquake.

Needs and Goals
Suppose you are a building inspector. You are checking some tall buildings. You want to see if the buildings will hold together during an earthquake.

Buildings built in a special way are less likely to shake apart.

Gathering Information
Earthquakes usually happen along fault lines. Most of the earth's fault lines are known. Builders can choose to put the building as far as possible from the fault.

1. The shaking of an earthquake goes through solid rock as short, sharp jolts. Soft, sandy ground makes waves like ocean water, and shakes more than solid rock. A tall building is better off on ground of solid rock. A short building might be safe on sandy ground if it is built with special supports.

2. Some buildings have an open ground floor, for example, a building with a garage underneath. Such a building sways at two different rates. The solid upper floors sway less. The flexible first floor sways more. The building could collapse.

3. A building whose long side is parallel (running in the same direction) to the fault will be less likely to sway.

4. A building whose long side is crosswise to the fault will sway much more.

5. An L-shaped building, which has one wing parallel to the fault and one wing running crosswise to the fault, will sway at different rates. The two wings may break apart.

Possible Alternatives

There are many building types. Imagine you are comparing the buildings shown here.

Evaluating Alternatives

Copy the table. Then examine each of the pictures on this page. Fill in information about each building in the correct row.

Making the Best Choice

Decide which building is the safest and would be damaged the least during an earthquake. Use your table to help you.

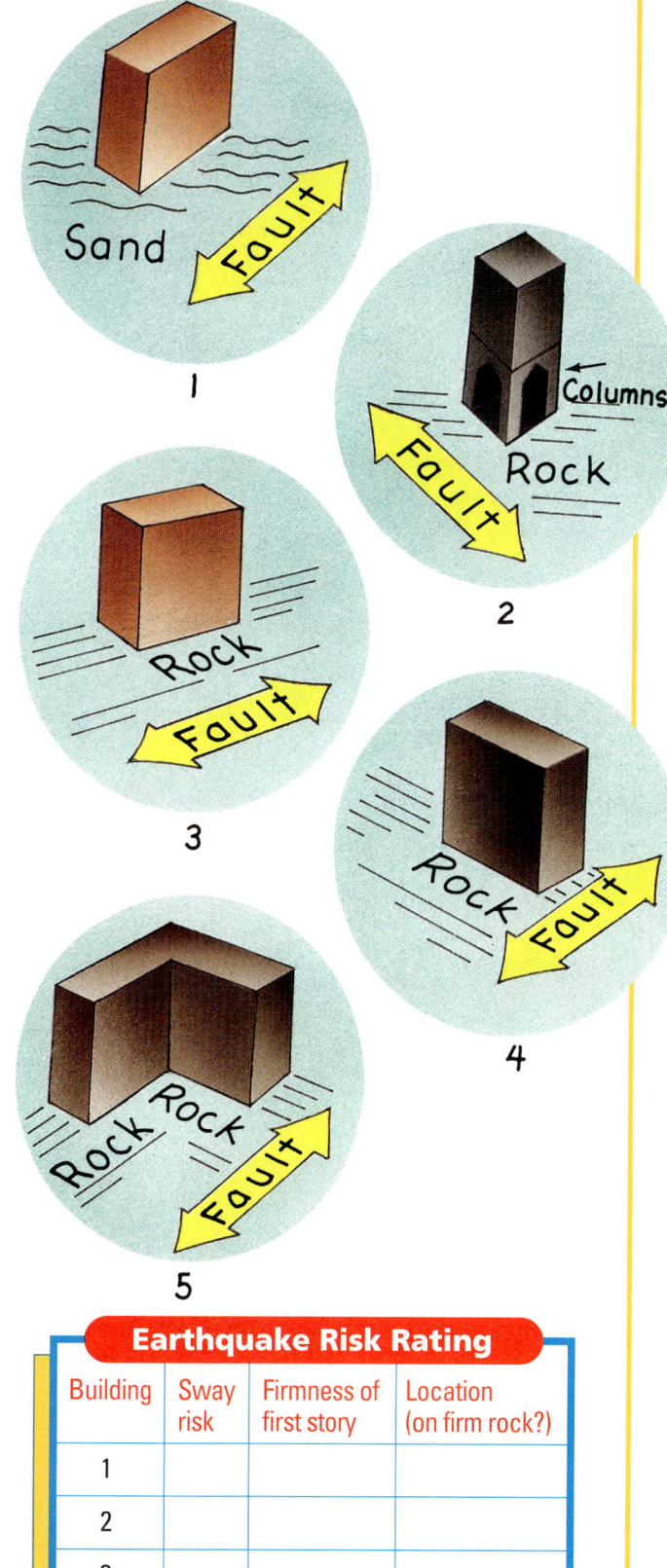

Now You Do It

1. Which building is the safest and would suffer the least damage in an earthquake? Why?

2. Which building seems almost as safe as the one you gave the top rating? Why?

3. *On Your Own* Look for pictures of buildings such as offices and schools. Of course, you can't tell whether they are built on sand or parallel to an earthquake fault. But examine things such as their height, whether they are L-shaped, and whether they have a solid first story. Tell whether they would be safe or unsafe in an earthquake zone.

4. *Critical Thinking* An earthquake is a natural disaster that can't be prevented. What preventable disasters do you know of? How can they be prevented?

Earthquake Risk Rating

Building	Sway risk	Firmness of first story	Location (on firm rock?)
1			
2			
3			
4			
5			

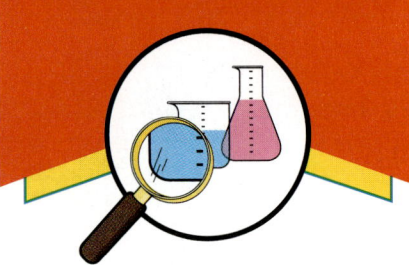

Reading the Quakes

Terri Hauk

Occupation: Seismologist
Current Project: *Expanding Your Horizons,* a program that encourages girls to become scientists

I n 1964, a huge earthquake struck Anchorage and Valdez in Alaska. Terri Hauk was fascinated by the reports on television. "Roads were breaking apart, a tidal wave formed a huge wall of water, and everything started shaking like a bowl of gelatin. Then one whole area sank into the ocean, houses and all. I was in awe of the forces of nature, and I wished that I could have helped to save those people's lives." Now Terri Hauk is a seismologist—she studies earthquakes.

How do you study earthquakes?

"I live near the San Andreas Fault in California. Tiny earthquakes happen there every single day. You wouldn't be able to feel them, but special instruments called seismometers measure the waves from each tiny quake. The tiny quakes are called tremors. I look for a pattern in the tremors—where they occur and how strong they are. Over time, these patterns and other data may show if the small tremors are related to the occurrences of large earthquakes."

When is the big one coming?

"We could save a lot of lives if we were able to predict exactly when an earthquake will hit. That's still the hard part. But we can do a lot just by knowing where an earthquake might hit and how strong it might be. We can say where it's not safe to build, and we can advise how strong a building should be to make it safe during earthquakes."

What do you like best about your job?

"It's good to know that my job helps other people, but I also like what I do every day in the lab. It's exciting to be a part of important research and to work with the top people in my field. There are new methods and new information. I'm learning something new every day."

Mining: Extracting Iron From Ore

Iron is found in a rock called iron ore. Once the iron is made pure, it is used to make steel. Iron and steel are used in almost every kind of machine.

1 Large pieces of iron ore are crushed into lumps or powder and sent to a tall tower called a blast furnace.

2 Ore and special chemicals are loaded into the top of the blast furnace.

3 Hot air is sent from stoves into the blast furnace. Chemical reactions occur. The iron melts and trickles down.

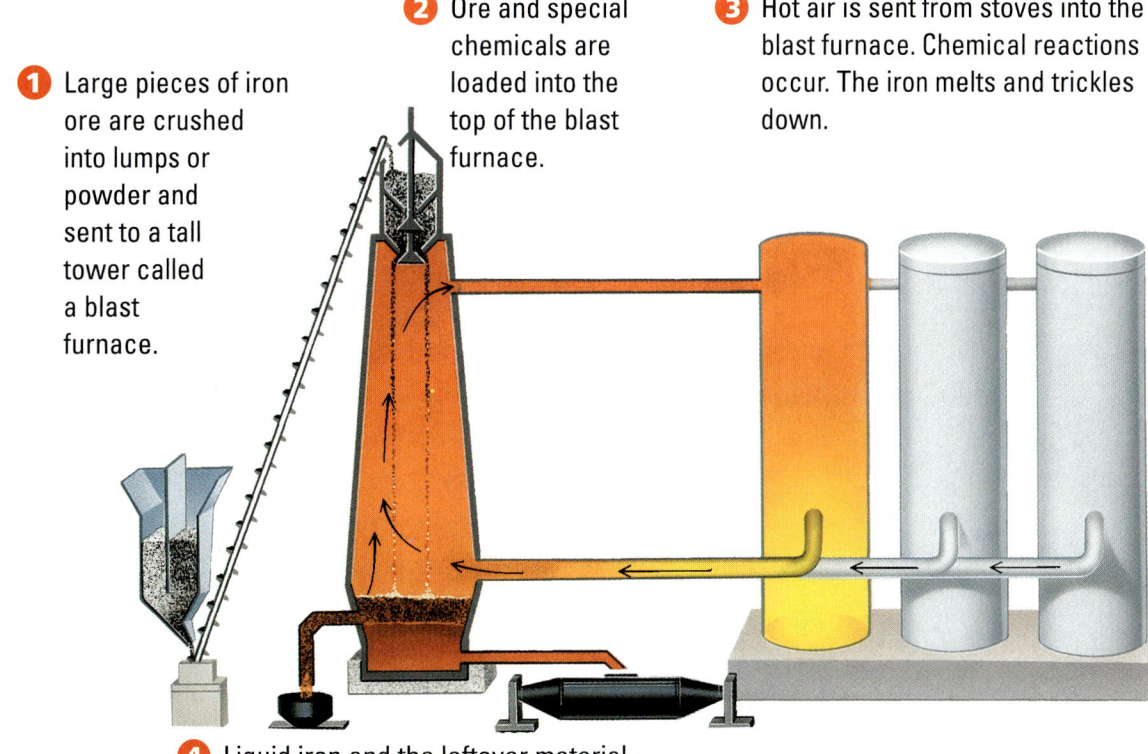

4 Liquid iron and the leftover material, called slag, are let out through different pipes at the bottom of the furnace.

Find Out On Your Own

Iron is one kind of ore. Use books to find out about other kinds of ores. List the ores, the metals found in them, and what the metals are used for.

Module Review

Making Connections

Energy

1. What causes magma to rise to the surface?

2. Explain what may make the plates of the earth move.

3. Explain why an earthquake occurs.

Patterns of Change

4. Explain two ways mountains form.

5. Name one instrument that scientists use to measure vibrations within Earth.

6. Explain why predicting earthquakes and volcanic eruptions is important.

Using What I Learned

Comparing

1. Explain how fault-block mountains and volcanoes are alike and different.

2. What is the difference between magma and lava?

Predicting

3. If you were a scientist and saw the lines on a seismograph move a great deal, what might you predict?

Categorizing

4. Name two differences between the Appalachian and Sierra Nevada Mountains.

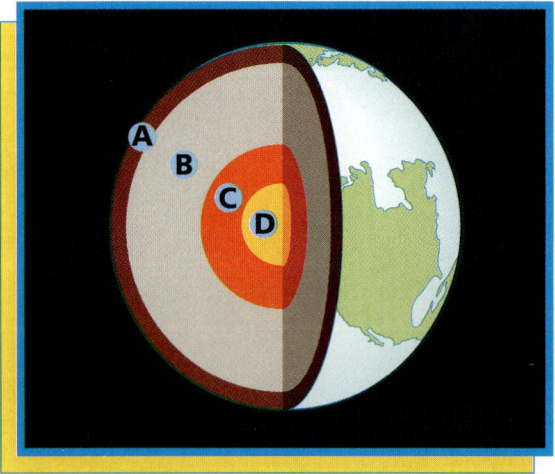

Communicating

5. Write a paragraph that describes how life returns to an area after a volcanic eruption.

Ordering

6. What is the correct order of the following layers of Earth from the outer part to the center: crust, inner core, mantle, outer core?

Relating

7. Why do scientists think that the Sierras are still rising?

Observing

8. Observe the diagram of the earth. In which layer, A, B, C, or D, are magma chambers found? Explain how magma chambers develop. Use the letters in the diagram in your explanation.

Applying What I Learned

Action Project
Find out about the results of earthquakes in other countries and the extent of damage caused by them. Contrast how the United States prepares its citizens for this type of disaster.

Drawing
Make a series of drawings to show what happens when a volcano erupts.

Science Theater
Write a TV news report describing either a volcanic eruption or an earthquake. Tell your viewers why this occurred, if there were any warning signs, and what they should do in the future to prepare for any similar occurrence.

Exhibition
Create a poster or bulletin board by drawing or tracing a large map of the United States. Find and label the major mountain ranges and the way in which they were formed.

What If
What if you read or heard that earthquakes were likely to occur in your area? What preparations might you make? How would you prepare others?

Performance Task
Use clay to show how folded mountains are formed and how fault-block mountains are formed.

Using Metric

About 1 centimeter

About 1 millimeter

About 1 meter

Water boils (100°C)

Normal body temperature (37°C)

Water freezes (0°C)

1 cm
1 cm

1 square centimeter

1 cm
1 cm
1 cm

1 cubic centimeter

About 1 kilogram

Degrees Celsius

11 football fields end to end is about 1 kilometer

1 liter of milk

Using Scientific Methods

Scientists ask many questions. No one may know the answers. Then scientists use scientific methods to find answers. Scientific methods include steps like those on the next page. Scientists sometimes use the steps in different order. You can use these steps to do the experiments in this section.

Test Hypothesis If possible, experiments are done to test the hypothesis. Experiments should be repeated to double check the results.

Collect Data The information you gather from the experiment is your data.

Study Data The data collected during an experiment is better understood if it is organized into charts and graphs. Then you can easily see what it all means.

Make Conclusions The conclusion relates to the hypothesis. You might conclude your hypothesis is correct, or that it is incorrect.

Identify Problem The problem is usually in the form of a question such as, "How much space does a bean plant need to grow best?"

Make Observations Recorded observations become data and might include the size, color, or shape of something.

State Hypothesis A hypothesis is a likely explanation of the problem. It may turn out to be incorrect; it must be tested.

Safety in Science

Scientists do their experiments safely. You need to be careful when doing experiments too. The next page includes some safety tips to remember.

- Read each experiment carefully.

- Wear cover goggles when needed.

- Clean up spills right away.

- Never taste or smell substances unless directed to do so by your teacher.

- Tape sharp edges of materials.

- Put things away when you finish an experiment.

- Wash your hands after each experiment.

Identifying a Problem

MODULE A

Experimenting with the Size of Splashes

Matt spilled some tomato juice when he poured a glass of juice for his little brother. Some juice landed on the table. More juice fell to the floor. Matt wondered why the splashes on the floor were much bigger than the splashes on the table.

Matt had identified a problem: What causes drops of a liquid to make splashes of different sizes? He knew that gravity was acting on all the drops. Gravity is the force that pulled the drops downward. Also, he believed that all the drops he spilled were about the same size. Matt decided to do an experiment to solve his problem.

Thinking About the Experiment

Matt could think of only one difference between the drops that hit the table and those that hit the floor. The drops that hit the floor had a greater distance to fall.

1. Which tomato juice drops fell from a greater distance?

2. Which tomato juice drops made bigger splashes?

3. What might Matt conclude from these observations?

In science class, Matt had learned that the variable being tested is the part of an experiment that changes. Also, a control is a part of the experiment that does not have the variable being tested.

4. What is the variable being tested in Matt's experiment on the next page?

5. What parts of Matt's experiment do not change?

Try It!

Try Matt's experiment and see if you come to the same conclusion.

Problem

What causes drops of a liquid to make splashes of different sizes?

Hypothesis

The size of the splash made by a drop is related to the distance the drop falls.

Materials

large sheet of
 white paper
cup
water
food coloring
dropper
meter stick

Procedure

1 Fill a cup halfway with water.

2 Add a few drops of food coloring to the water.

3 Lay the paper on the floor.

4 Fill the dropper halfway with colored water.

5 Stand the meter stick up on the paper. Set the stick so it is near one end of the paper. Hold the dropper 25 cm above the paper.

6 Drop 1 drop of colored water on the paper from a height of 25 cm. Write 25 cm on the paper next to the splash.

7 Move the stick a small distance away from the splash.

8 Repeat steps 5 and 6 at heights of 50 cm and 100 cm. After each drop, write the height of the drop next to the splash. Then move the meter stick so there is space on the paper for the next drop.

Data and Observations

Tell what happened to the size of the splash. In a chart like the one below, write: small, bigger, biggest.

Distance	Size of splash
25 cm	
50 cm	
100 cm	

Conclusion

Write your conclusion based on your data and observations.

Practice

Identifying a Problem

1. Suppose you wanted to do an experiment that compared the thickness of liquids to the size of their splashes. Identify the problem you would want to solve in your experiment.

2. How would you change Matt's experiment to solve this problem?

Testing a Hypothesis

Experimenting with Gravity

When the noon bell rang, Tom dropped his apple core into an empty paper cup. On the way out of the lunch room, he pitched the paper cup into a wastebasket. He noticed that the apple core stayed in the cup and landed in the basket—still inside the cup. Tom wondered why the apple core did not fly out of the cup before the cup hit the basket.

Tom had observed many falling objects. He wondered about how the force of gravity affects objects that are falling at the same time. He thought that objects falling together fall at the same rate.

Tom decided to set up an experiment with falling objects. He watched a cup of water fall. Then he poked holes in another cup. He put water into this cup and observed it as it fell.

Thinking About the Experiment
Tom dropped a cup and water to test his hypothesis. He observed the rate at which each fell.

1. What was Tom's hypothesis?

2. What might Tom have observed if the water fell slower than the cup? faster?

Tom observed that water did not flow out of cup 2 when the holes were uncovered and the cup was dropped.

3. What does this tell you about the rate at which the water and cup fell?

4. What does this tell you about Tom's hypothesis?

Try It!

Try Tom's experiment and see if you come to the same conclusion.

....

Problem

How does the force of gravity affect objects falling together?

Hypothesis

Write your own hypothesis for this experiment.

Materials

2 paper cups
  of the same size
sink or large pail

pencil
tap water
meter stick

Procedure

1 Label the cups *1* and *2*.

2 Fill cup *1* half full of water.

3 Hold the cup at least 1 m above a sink or pail. Let go of the cup and observe what happens to it and the water as the cup falls. Record your observations.

4 Use the point of a pencil to make two small holes near the center of the bottom of cup *2*.

5 Cover the holes in the cup with your fingers. Then fill cup *2* halfway with water.

6 Hold the cup at least 1 m above a sink or pail. Take your finger off the holes. Observe what happens to the water. Record your observations.

7 Again fill cup *2* half full of water, holding your fingers over the holes. Hold the cup over a sink or pail. Uncover the holes as you let go of the cup. Observe what happens to the water and the cup as the cup falls. Record your observations.

Data and Observations

Situation	Observations
Cup 1 (falling)	
Cup 2 (held)	
Cup 2 (falling)	

Conclusion

Write your conclusion based on your data and observations.

Practice

Testing a Hypothesis

Suppose you wanted to find out how the force of gravity affects the water in a cup with holes on the side.

1. What would your hypothesis be?

2. How could you set up an experiment to test your hypothesis?

3. What experiment results would support your hypothesis?

Setting Up a Control

MODULE B

Experimenting with Salt Water

Alex was on a vacation with his family. He noticed that it seemed easier to float in the ocean than in the pool back home. Alex knew that ocean water has salt in it. His pool was filled with water from a faucet. This water is fresh water and is not salty.

Alex wondered if things float more easily in salt water than in fresh water. Alex decided to set up an experiment to find out. He filled a cup with salt water. Alex added drops of colored fresh water, vinegar, and rubbing alcohol to the salt water. Alex then watched to see whether the drops floated or sank.

Thinking About the Experiment

Review what Alex wanted to do.

1. What was the problem Alex wanted to solve?

2. Write a hypothesis for the problem.

Alex did not set up his experiment correctly. He did not have a control. The control is the part of the experiment that does not have the variable being tested.

3. Could Alex compare whether the liquids floated more easily in salt water than in fresh water? Explain.

4. What type of water should have been the control?

5. Read Alex's experiment on the next page. How did Alex correct his experiment to have a control?

Try It!

Try Alex's experiment and see if you come to the same conclusion.

Problem

Do things float more easily in salt water than in fresh water?

Hypothesis

Write your own hypothesis for this experiment.

Materials

graduated cylinder   white vinegar
salt   rubbing alcohol
food coloring   1 small plastic cup
water   3 droppers
2 large plastic cups   spoon

Procedure

1 Label one large cup *Fresh water* and the other large cup *Salt water.*

2 Add 200 mL of tap water to each of the large cups.

3 Pour 50 mL of salt into the cup labeled *Salt water.* Stir the salt until it dissolves.

4 Pour 5 mL of fresh water into the small cup. Add several drops of food coloring.

5 Add one or two drops of the colored water to the *Fresh water* cup. Observe what happens to the drops.

6 Now add one or two drops of the colored water to the *Salt water* cup. Observe what happens to the drops. Rinse all the cups.

7 Repeat steps 2 through 6, using colored vinegar instead of colored water in the small cup.

8 Repeat steps 2 through 6, using colored alcohol instead of colored water in the small cup.

Data and Observations

Do the drops mix, float, or sink?

	Fresh water	Salt water
Water		
Alcohol		
Vinegar		

Conclusion

Write your conclusion based on your data and observations.

Practice

Setting Up a Control

You might want to design an experiment to test if solid objects float more easily in water than in other liquids.

1. What would be your control in this experiment?

2. What would be the variable that changes in this experiment?

3. What are some liquids other than water you could use?

Testing a Hypothesis

MODULE B

Experimenting with Brine Shrimp

Terry went to a pet store to get some brine shrimp to feed to his fish. He enjoyed looking at all the fish while he was there. Terry noticed that the store owner kept brine shrimp in an aquarium under bright light. He wondered why. He thought of a hypothesis to explain what he noticed: Brine shrimp like light places more than dark places. Terry decided to do an experiment to test his hypothesis.

He bought some brine shrimp and put them in a clear plastic jar. He cut a small hole in a piece of black paper. He wrapped the paper around the jar so that the hole would let light into part of the jar. Then he shined a flashlight through the hole. He took off the paper and observed the brine shrimp.

Thinking About the Experiment

Terry made an observation in the pet store that made him wonder about brine shrimp. Then he thought of a hypothesis.

1. What did Terry notice?

2. What was Terry's hypothesis?

To test his hypothesis, Terry first put the hole in the paper near the bottom of a jar and made observations. Then he moved the hole near the top of the jar and made observations.

3. How did using black paper help Terry test his hypothesis?

4. Why was it important for him to shine the light in two different places?

5. If the brine shrimp had gathered only at the bottom of the jar, would Terry's hypothesis have been correct? Why?

Try It!

Try Terry's experiment and see if you come to the same conclusion.

Problem

Do brine shrimp like light places or dark places?

Hypothesis

Brine shrimp like light places more than dark places.

Materials

20 brine shrimp   scissors
plastic jar   flashlight
black paper   clock or watch
tape   with second hand

Procedure

1 Put the brine shrimp and salt water in a clear plastic jar.

2 Cut a piece of black paper large enough to wrap around the jar. Cut a small square out of one edge of the paper.

3 Wrap the paper around the jar so that the square hole is near the bottom of the jar. Use tape to hold the paper in place. If the lid of the jar is clear, cover it with black paper.

4 Shine the flashlight through the hole for about 1 minute.

5 Quickly remove the paper and observe where the brine shrimp are. Record your observations in a chart like the one below.

6 Repeat steps 3-5, but position the paper so the square hole is near the top of the jar.

Data and Observations

	Position of Shrimp
Light at bottom	
Light at top	

Conclusion

Write your conclusion based on your data and observations.

Practice

Testing a Hypothesis

1. Suppose you put some warm salt water in the jar. Then you put a funnel in the warm water and pour cold salt water through the funnel. When you remove the funnel, the cold salt water will stay under the warm salt water. You put brine shrimp in the jar and observe their behavior. What is the variable being tested in this new procedure?

2. What hypothesis are you testing?

Setting Up an Experiment

Experimenting with Erosion

Robin lives where winter brings ice and snow. One spring, she saw that some soil had washed away from the hill behind her house. No soil had washed away in her front yard. Her front yard was flat. Robin wondered whether the slope of the land affected the amount of erosion caused by melting ice and snow. She thought it did.

Robin wanted to do an experiment to find out. She needed a way to set up models of flat land and a hill. She decided to use damp sand for soil. She found two lids from shoe boxes to hold the sand. She decided to use ice cubes for melting ice and snow.

Thinking About the Experiment

1. What is the problem that Robin wants to solve?

2. Write a hypothesis for the problem.

The experiment on the next page describes how Robin set up her experiment. She kept every part of the setup the same except for one part. This part is the variable she wanted to test.

3. What parts of the setup are the same for each model?

4. What is the variable Robin's setup tests?

Robin also has a control in her experiment. The control is the part of the setup that shows what happens when ice melts on soil that has no slope.

5. Which part of the setup is the control?

6. What does the part of the setup with the hill of sand test?

Try It!

Try Robin's experiment and see if you come to the same conclusion.

Problem

Does the slope of land affect the amount of erosion caused by melting ice?

Hypothesis

Write your own hypothesis for this experiment.

Materials

2 lids from shoe boxes
aluminum foil
damp sand
2 ice cubes

Procedure

1 Cover the inside of both lids with foil to make them waterproof.

2 Fill each lid with the same amount of damp sand.

3 In 1 lid, shape a steep hill.

4 Smooth out the sand in the other lid so that it is flat.

5 Place 1 ice cube on top of the hill. Place another ice cube in the middle of the flat sand.

6 Watch as the ice melts in each lid. Record your observations in a chart like the one below.

Data and Observations

	Amount of Erosion
Flat land	
Hill	

Conclusion

Write your conclusion based on your data and observations.

Practice

Setting Up an Experiment

1. If you wanted to set up an experiment to find out how the slope of land affects erosion caused by rain, what would be your hypothesis?

2. Describe how you would set up the experiment to test your hypothesis.

Using Models

MODULE C

Experimenting with Properties of Liquids and Solids

Tim's science class was studying earthquakes. He learned that the earth's plates float on partly melted rock, which is located deep inside the earth. This partly melted rock makes up a layer of the earth called the asthenosphere.

Tim read that the asthenosphere is subjected to tremendous pressure and heat. Because of these conditions, rock in the asthenosphere can flow like a very thick liquid.

Tim searched for some ordinary material that shows properties of both a liquid and a solid. He wanted to use this material to make a model of the asthenosphere. He learned that adding water to cornstarch creates a substance with unusual properties. He decided to use cornstarch for his model.

Thinking About the Experiment

In order for a model to be useful, it must show how something looks or works. Scientists use models to describe ideas about nature. They often use a model to represent something, such as the asthenosphere, which they cannot see directly.

1. In the procedure on the next page, describe the point where the mixture best represents the asthenosphere.

2. Would the model be more like a liquid or a solid in step 3? in step 6?

3. What would the nail show?

4. In what part of the procedure could the model be compared to the asthenosphere under pressure?

Try It!

Try Tim's experiment and see if you come to the same conclusion.

Problem

Do some materials have properties of both liquids and solids?

Hypothesis

Some materials have properties of both liquids and solids.

Materials

balance	clear plastic cup
cornstarch, (40 g)	graduated cylinder
nail	spoon
water	

Procedure

1 Pour 15 mL of water into a cup.

2 Mix 10 g of cornstarch in the cup.

3 Place the nail head-first on the surface of the mixture. Observe the consistency of the mixture and whether it can support the nail. Record your observations.

4 Add 5 g more of cornstarch to the bowl and stir until it is mixed. Repeat step 3.

5 Repeat step 4 until the mixture is thick enough to be scooped up and rolled into a small ball. Record your observations.

6 Put the ball of cornstarch mixture in the palm of your hand. Let it warm on your palm for several minutes. Record any changes you see.

7 Remold the mixture into a ball. Apply gentle pressure to the ball for several minutes. Observe and record how the ball responds to pressure.

Data and Observations

Amount of cornstarch	Texture of mixture	Effect on nail
10 g		
15 g		
20 g		
25 g		
30 g		

	Changes in ball shape
In palm	
With pressure	

Conclusion

Write your conclusion based on your data and observations.

Practice

Using Models

Suppose you wanted to find out if a mixture of flour and water has the properties of both a liquid and a solid and can be used to make a model of the asthenosphere.

1. What would be your hypothesis?
2. How would you set up an experiment to test your hypothesis?
3. What would be the model in the experiment?

Setting Up an Experiment

Experimenting with Yeast

Glen was helping his aunt make bread. The recipe called for yeast. His aunt told him that yeast are one-celled organisms. They use an ingredient in the recipe for food. When they use food, they make a gas that causes the bread dough to rise. Glen wondered what ingredient the yeast use for food. The recipe listed flour, sugar, salt, water, eggs, and yeast. Glen wondered if yeast might use sugar for food.

He decided to set up an experiment to find out if yeast use sugar. Since yeast make a gas when they use food, he decided to set up an experiment that would show if gas was given off. By putting balloons over the mouths of jars, Glen can tell if the yeast are using food. The gas they make will help blow up the balloons.

Thinking About the Experiment

1. What is the problem that Glen wants to solve?

2. Write a hypothesis for the problem.

Read Glen's experiment carefully. He kept every part of the setup the same except for one part. This part is the variable he was testing.

3. What did he put in each jar?

4. What parts of the setup are the same for each jar?

5. What is the variable that changes in the setup?

Glen also has a control in his experiment. The control is the part of the setup that shows what happens to the balloon when yeast do not have any food.

6. Which part of the setup is the control?

7. What does the part of the setup with sugar test?

Try It!

Try Glen's experiment and see if you come to the same conclusion.

Problem

What do yeast use for food?

Hypothesis

Write your own hypothesis for this experiment.

Materials

2 identical jars with small mouths
cover goggles
tape
spoonful of sugar

2 spoonfuls of yeast
20 mL warm water
2 balloons

Procedure

1 Put a piece of tape on each of the jars. Write *No food* on 1 piece of tape. Write *Sugar* on another piece of tape.

2 Put a spoonful of sugar in the jar labeled *Sugar*.

3 Put a spoonful of yeast in each jar.

4 Add 10 mL of warm water to each jar.

5 Stretch a balloon over the mouth of each jar.

6 Place the jars in a warm, dark place for the night.

7 The next day observe the balloons. Record the observations in a chart like the one below.

Data and Observations

Descriptions of balloons

	Changes in balloons
Sugar	
No food	

Conclusion

Write your conclusion based on your data and observations.

Practice

Setting Up an Experiment

1. If you wanted to do an experiment to find out if yeast use sugar or corn syrup better as food, what might be your hypothesis?

2. Describe how you would set up the experiment to test your hypothesis.

Testing a Hypothesis

Experimenting with Water

Tina was getting ice cubes from the freezer. She noticed that the water in the tray that had been filled with water was not frozen. The water in the tray that had been only half full was frozen. Tina remembered that during the winter small ponds freeze sooner than larger lakes. In both examples, the water that did not freeze as fast had a larger volume. Tina decided that a larger volume of water cools more slowly than a smaller volume of water.

Tina wanted to test her hypothesis. She decided to use a large and a small jar to stand for a pond and a lake. She used a thermometer to measure how fast warm water cooled in each jar.

Thinking About the Experiment

The experiment on the next page describes how Tina tested her hypothesis.

1. How are the two jars of water alike?

2. How are they different?

3. Tina could have tested her hypothesis using two jars of the same size. Explain how the jars could still have different volumes.

4. Why did Tina begin with warm water?

In an experiment, the part that is different between setups is the variable being tested.

5. What variable is being tested in Tina's experiment?

6. Why did Tina measure the water temperature in both jars at the same time?

Try It!

Try Tina's experiment and see if you come to the same conclusion.

Problem

How does the amount of water affect how fast the water loses heat?

Hypothesis

A larger volume of water cools more slowly than a smaller volume does.

Materials

1 small plastic jar   warm tap water
l large plastic jar   clock or watch
2 thermometers   with second hand

Procedure

1   Fill both jars with warm tap water.

2   Place each jar on a flat surface, about 15 cm apart.

3   Place a thermometer in each jar.

4   Use a clock or watch to time each minute.

5   Read the water temperature in each jar once each minute for the next 10 minutes. Record the temperatures in a chart like the one shown.

Data and Observations

Time in minutes	Temperature in ˚C	
	Large jar	Small jar
0		
1		
2		
3		
4		
5		
6		
7		
8		
9		
10		

Conclusion

Write your conclusion based on your data and observations.

Practice

Testing a Hypothesis

Another experiment would be needed to find out if large bodies of water warm up faster than smaller ones.

1. Write a hypothesis for this experiment.

2. How could you change the experiment above to test this hypothesis?

Setting Up an Experiment

Experimenting with Evaporation

Julie's science class made salt solutions on Friday. When the bell rang, the students put their jars of solution in a cupboard. Julie left her jar on a sunny windowsill in the classroom.

On Monday, Julie found that only salt crystals were left in her jar. The water had evaporated from her solution. She noticed that the jars in the cupboard still contained solutions. Julie decided that the warm temperature on the windowsill caused her solution to evaporate quickly.

She set up an experiment to see how temperature affects the evaporation of salt water. She left jars of salt water open to air at different temperatures.

Thinking About the Experiment

Julie knew that water slowly disappears if it is left in an open container.

1. What happened to the water in Julie's solution?

2. How could she have kept her solution from evaporating?

3. Could Julie have set up her experiment, shown on the next page, using tap water instead of salt water? Explain.

Julie set up her experiment so that only one thing is different for the jars. The part of the experiment that is different is the variable being tested.

4. What is the same for each jar?

5. What is the variable begin tested in Julie's experiment?

Julie has a control in her experiment. In this experiment, the control is the part of the setup that shows how fast water evaporates in Julie's classroom. Note procedure step 4.

6. Which part of the setup is the control?

Try Julie's experiment and see if you come to the same conclusion.

Problem

Does the temperature of the air have an effect on how fast salt water evaporates from an open container?

Hypothesis

Salt water evaporates faster in warm air than in cold air.

Materials

3 jars of same size	water
salt	marker
spoon	200-watt lamp
graduated cylinder	and stand

Procedure

1 Use the marker to label the 3 jars *A*, *B*, and *C*.

2 Prepare a salt solution by dissolving 5 mL of salt in 60 mL of warm water.

3 Pour 20 mL of the salt solution into each of the 3 jars. Mark the water level on the side of each jar.

4 Set jar *A* under the lighted lamp. Place jar *B* somewhere in the room where it will not be disturbed. Set jar *C* in a cold place. Make sure none of the jars is in a drafty place.

5 Check the jars at the end of each day for 3 days. Record your observations in a chart like the one below.

Data and Observations

Day	Water level		
	A	**B**	**C**
1			
2			
3			

Conclusion

Write your conclusion based on your data and observations.

Practice

Setting Up an Experiment

Suppose you want to find out how air temperature affects the evaporation of a liquid other than salt water.

1. What liquid would you use?
2. What might be your hypothesis?
3. How would you set up an experiment to test your hypothesis?

Making Conclusions

MODULE E

Experimenting with Cotton Thread and Humidity

Jennifer liked to curl her naturally straight hair. She noticed that on dry, cold days her hair stayed curly. On hot, humid days, her curls became looser. Jennifer asked her teacher if human hair shows how much moisture is in the air. The teacher explained that an instrument called a hair hygrometer measures humidity. The hair hygrometer works because hair stretches out when the air becomes humid. The hair absorbs moisture from the air.

Jennifer wondered if she could make a hygrometer from cotton thread. She wondered if the thread would measure relative humidity accurately. She made this hypothesis to answer her question: *A cotton thread hygrometer accurately measures changes in relative humidity.* Jennifer set up an experiment to test her hypothesis.

Thinking About the Experiment

Jennifer collected data in her experiment. She used the data to make a conclusion about the accuracy of her hypothesis. She studied the data to decide if it supported her hypothesis.

1. In the procedure on the next page, what did Jennifer observe to test her hypothesis?

2. On what data would she base her conclusion?

3. What would Jennifer's data and observations have to show in order to support her hypothesis?

The length of the cotton thread did not change. Jennifer concluded that the data she collected did not support her hypothesis.

4. What kind of data would make her conclude that her hypothesis is false?

5. Why did Jennifer need to know the relative humidity of the air?

Try It!

Try Jennifer's experiment and see if you come to the same conclusion.

Problem

Can a cotton thread hygrometer accurately measure changes in the relative humidity of air?

Hypothesis

Recall that Jennifer's hypothesis was incorrect. Write your own hypothesis for this experiment.

Materials

pencil
scissors
transparent tape
cotton thread, 20 cm long

metric ruler
shoe box
small nail
paper, 2 cm x 3 cm

Procedure

1 Fasten the head end of the nail to one end of the thread with small pieces of tape.

2 Tape the other end of the thread to the inside bottom of the shoe box. Tape the thread so it is centered near one end of the box.

3 Stand the shoe box on its end so the thread hangs straight down the middle of the box.

4 Use the ruler to measure 25 mm on the edge of the paper. Mark off every millimeter on the line. Label every 5 mm, starting at 0 mm.

5 Tape the scale to the bottom of the shoe box, beside the nail. The tip of the nail should touch the 13 mm mark.

6 Every day for 5 days record the position of the nail tip on the scale. Try to make your measurements at the same time of day. Record your measurements on a chart like the one shown.

7 Get the actual relative humidity from a local weather report for each time you record the nail's position. Record the actual relative humidity on your chart.

Data and Observations

Date	Position of nail tip	Relative humidity

Conclusion

Write your conclusion based on your data and observations.

Practice

Making Conclusions
Suppose you wanted to test materials other than cotton thread for making a hygrometer.
1. What other materials might you use?
2. If you tested one of those materials and found that during high humidity the materials sometimes got shorter and sometimes got longer, what might you conclude?

Making Conclusions

MODULE F

Experimenting with Grape Ivy Leaves

Shannon visited a sunny greenhouse. She bought a grape ivy plant. The woman at the greenhouse told her that this kind of plant grows best when it gets a lot of light.

When Shannon got home, she began to wonder what would happen to the plant's leaves if they did not get enough light. Before she could make any conclusions, she would need to do an experiment. Shannon chose a large healthy branch with six leaves on it. She taped squares of black paper to the front and back of each leaf. She left the plant near a sunny window.

Thinking About the Experiment

1. Why did Shannon cover some of the leaves?

2. Why did Shannon not cover all of the leaves on the plant?

After a week, Shannon removed the paper from the leaves. Three leaves had turned yellow. Two others had yellow spots. The sixth leaf was a pale green.

3. Should Shannon have concluded that her hypothesis was wrong since one covered leaf still looked green? Explain.

4. What part of Shannon's data supported her hypothesis?

5. What conclusion do you think Shannon reached?

Suppose that Shannon had observed no changes in the leaves that were covered for a week.

6. Would that data support her hypothesis? Explain.

7. What conclusion would Shannon have made based on that data?

Try It!

Try Shannon's experiment and see if you come to the same conclusion.

Problem

What happens to grape ivy leaves when they do not get enough light?

Hypothesis

Leaves of grape ivy plants will not stay green if they do not get enough light.

Materials

2 sheets of black paper
scissors

grape ivy plant
tape
water

Procedure

1 Choose a branch of the plant with 5 or 6 healthy leaves on it.

2 Cut 2 squares of black paper for each leaf on the branch. The squares should be big enough to cover the leaves completely.

3 Tape 2 squares together along 1 edge. Slip a leaf between the 2 squares. Then tape the other edge of the squares together.

4 Put the plant in a sunny place and water it normally.

5 After 1 week, remove the paper from the leaves.

6 Using a chart like the one shown, record how the leaves look.

Data and Observations

	Appearance of leaves
Covered leaves	
Leaves with no color	

Conclusion

Write your conclusion based on your data and observations.

Practice

Making Conclusions

1. If you wanted to experiment to find out if white paper squares block out the same amount of light as black paper squares, how would you change the procedure?

2. If leaves covered with white squares showed no changes, what conclusion would you make?

Glossary

A

adaptation (ad′ap tā′shən), a structure or behavior that helps a living thing live in its surroundings.

adapted (ə dap′tid), made fit to live under certain conditions.

air mass, a large amount of air with the same temperature and humidity.

air pressure (presh′ər), the amount that air presses or pushes on anything.

air resistance (ri zis′təns), a force that slows down the movement of objects through the air.

altitude (al′tə tüd), the height above sea level.

anemometer (an′ə mom′ə tər), a tool that measures wind speed.

asteroid (as′tə roid′), a rocky object orbiting the sun between the planets.

asteroid (as′tə roid′) **belt,** a large group of rocks that orbit the sun between Mars and Jupiter.

atmosphere (at′mə sfir), the layer of gases that surrounds the earth.

atom (at′əm), a basic bit of matter.

axis (ak′sis), an imaginary line through a spinning object.

B

barometer (bə rom′ə tər), an instrument that measures air pressure.

Beaufort (bō′fərt) **scale,** a scale used to estimate wind speed based on observing objects moving in the environment.

biosphere (bī′ə sfir), the region on and surrounding the earth that can support life and that includes the atmosphere, water, and soil.

C

Calorie (kal′ər ē), a specific amount of energy in food.

carbon dioxide (dī ok′sīd), a gas in air that is taken in by plants, exhaled by animals, and given off when fuel is burned.

Celsius (sel′sē əs) **degree,** a unit for measuring temperature.

central vent (sen′trəl vent), a large hole through which magma bursts out of a volcano.

cirrus (sir′əs) **cloud,** a white, feathery cloud made up of tiny pieces of ice.

climate (klī′mit), the average weather conditions of an area over many years.

cold front, the area where a cold air mass moves toward a warm air mass and pushes the warm air up quickly.

colonizer (kol′ə nīz ər), a living thing that comes into an area to eat and live.

comet (kom′it), a frozen chunk of ice and dust that orbits the sun.

compressed (kəm prest′) **air,** air put under extra pressure or squeezed so that it takes up less space.

condense (kən dens′), to change from a gas to a liquid.

conservation (kon′sər vā′shən), protecting from loss or from being used up.

consumer (kən sü′mər), a living thing that depends on producers for food.

contract (kən trakt′), to become smaller in size or to move closer together.

control (kən trol′), the part of an experiment that does not have the variable being tested.

convection (kən vek′shən) **currents,** the circular movement of gases or liquids as a result of differences in temperature.

core (kôr), the center part of the earth.

crust (krust), the top layer of the earth.

cumulonimbus (kyü′myə lō nim′bəs) **cloud,** a cloud that looks like a tall, dark cumulus cloud and often brings thunderstorms.

cumulus (kyü′myə ləs) **cloud,** a white, fluffy cloud that looks like cotton.

D

dark zone, the ocean waters between 1200 and 4000 meters deep where sunlight does not reach.

deciduous (di sij′ü əs) **tree,** one of a group of trees that lose their leaves in the fall.

decomposer (dē′kəm pō′zər), a consumer that puts materials from dead plants and animals back into soil, air, and water.

dissolve (di zolv′), to spread evenly in a liquid and form a solution.

Doppler (dop′lər) **radar,** a type of radar that shows distance and direction of movement.

E

earthquake (ėrth′kwāk), a shaking or sliding of the earth's crust.

ecosystem (ē′kō sis′təm), a community and its nonliving environment.

ellipse (i lips′), the shape of a circle that has been flattened a little.

erosion (i rō′zhən), the moving of weathered rocks and soil by wind, water, or ice.

eruption (i rup′shən), the bursting forth or flowing of lava from a volcano.

evacuate (i vak′yü āt), to withdraw from.

evaporate (i vap′ə rāt′), to change from a liquid to a gas.

evergreen, a plant that stays green all year, including firs and pines.

extinct (ek stingkt′), something that is no longer found living on earth.

F

fault (fôlt), a crack in the earth's crust along which rocks move.

fault-block mountain, a mountain that forms when a big block of rock moves up along a fault.

folded mountain, a mountain that forms when two plates in the earth's crust collide and the edges of the plates crumple.

food chain, the path that energy and nutrients take in a community.

force (fôrs), a push or a pull.

fossil (fos′əl), a trace of a plant or animal that is often found in sedimentary rock.

front, the line where two air masses meet.

G

gas, a state of matter with no definite shape or volume.

geyser (gī′zer), a spring that spouts a fountain or jet of hot water and steam into the air.

glacier (glā′shər), a large mass of ice that moves very slowly.

glider (glī′dər), a motorless aircraft that is kept in the air by rising air currents.

graduated cylinder (graj′ü āt ed sil′ən dər), piece of equipment used for measuring volume.

gravitational force (grav′ə tā′shə nəl fôrs), the pull of gravity that causes all the planets to orbit around the sun.

gravity (grav′ə tē), a force that pulls any two objects together.

greenhouse effect, the trapping of heat by the air around the earth.

H

habitat (hab′ə tat), the place where a living thing lives.

high-pressure area, an area where cool air sinks and pushes down on the earth with more pressure.

Homo sapiens (hō′mō sā′pē enz), the species including all existing races of human beings.

hot spot, a place in the earth's mantle where the mantle melts because of extreme heat.

humidity (hyü mid′ə tē), the amount of water vapor in the air.

hurricane (hėr′ə kān), a huge storm that forms over a warm ocean and has strong winds and heavy rains.

hydrogen (hī′drə jən), a colorless, odorless, gaseous element that burns easily and has less mass than any other element.

hydrosphere (hī′drə sfir), the water portion of the earth.

hygrometer (hī grom′ə tər), an instrument that measures humidity.

hypothesis (hī poth′ə sis), a likely explanation of a problem.

J

jet propulsion (prə pul′shən), a forward motion produced by the reaction of an object to high-pressure gas moving in the opposite direction.

L

lava (lä′və), hot, melted rock that flows from a volcano.

lift (lift), an upward movement.

light zone, the sunlit waters from the ocean surface down to 100 meters.

liquid, a state of matter with a definite volume but no definite shape.

lithosphere (lith′ə sfir), the solid portion of the earth.

low-pressure area, an area where warm air rises and pushes down on the earth with less pressure.

lunar eclipse (lü′nər i klips′), the darkening of the moon as it passes through the earth's shadow.

M

magma (mag′mə), hot, melted rock deep inside the earth.

magma chamber (mag′mə chām′bər), a large, underground lake of magma in the earth's crust.

mantle (man′tl), the earth's middle layer.

mass (mas), the amount of material that an object has in it.

meteor (mē′tē ər), a piece of rock or dust from space burning up in the earth's air.

meteorite (mē′tē ə rīt′), a rock from space that has passed through the air and landed on the ground.

meteorologist (mē′tē ə rol′e jist), a person who studies weather.

mineral (min′ər əl), nonliving solid matter from the earth.

mixture (miks′cher), two or more substances that are placed together but can be easily separated.

molecule (mol′ə kyül), two or more atoms held together.

moraine (mə rān′), a mass or ridge made of rocks, dirt, etc, that were scraped up and deposited by a glacier.

N

nutrient (nü′trē ənt), a material that plants and animals need to live and grow.

O

Oort Cloud, a vast cloud of comets that might exist in space billions of kilometers past the outermost planet.

orbit (ôr′bit), the path of an object around another object.

oxygen (ok′sə jən), a gas that is given off by plants and used by animals.

ozone (ō′zōn) **layer,** the region of concentrated ozone that shields the earth from excessive ultraviolet radiation.

P

pectoral (pek′tər əl) **muscles,** chest muscles.

planet (plan′it), a large body of matter revolving around the sun.

plankton (plangk′tən), the small organisms that float or drift in water, especially at or near the surface.

plate, one of twenty sections of solid rock that make up the earth's crust.

polar climate (pō′lər klī′mit), a major climate zone that receives indirect sunlight all year and that has cold or cool temperatures all year.

pollination (pol′li na′shən), the movement of pollen from a stamen to a pistil.

pollution (pə lü′shən), the addition of harmful substances to land, air, or water.

precipitation (pri sip′ə tā′shən), moisture that falls to the ground from clouds.

pressure (presh′ər), the force exerted on a certain area.

producer (prə dü′sər), a living thing that can use sunlight to make sugars.

property (prop′ər tē), something about an object that can be observed, such as size or shape.

R

rain gauge (gāj), an instrument that measures precipitation.

rainforest, a very dense forest in a region, usually tropical, where rain is very heavy throughout the year.

recycle (rē sī′kəl), to change something so it can be reused.

reef (rēf), narrow ridge of rocks, sand, or coral at or near the surface of the water.

revolution (rev′ə lü′shən), the movement of one object around another object.

rotation (rō tā′shən), one full spin of an object around an axis.

S

saliva (sə lī′və), the fluid in the mouth that makes chewed food wet and begins digestion.

saturated (sach′ə rā′tid) **air,** air that contains all the water vapor it can possibly hold.

season (sē′zn), one of the four periods of the year—spring, summer, fall, or winter.

sedimentary (sed′ə men′tər ē) **rock,** rock made of sediments that have been pressed together.

seismograph (sīz′mə graf), an instrument for recording the direction, strength, and time of earthquakes or other movements of the earth's crust.

solar eclipse (sō′lər i klips′), the blocking of sunlight by the moon as the moon passes between the sun and the earth.

solar system, the sun, the nine planets and their moons, and other objects that orbit the sun.

solid, a state of matter with a definite shape and a definite volume.

solstice (sol′stis), either of the two times in the year when the sun is at its greatest distance from the equator and appears to be farthest north or south in the sky.

solution (sə lü′shən), a mixture in which one substance spreads evenly throughout another substance.

sonic (son′ik) **boom,** a loud noise caused by an airplane crossing through the sound barrier when it travels faster than the speed of sound.

species (spē′shēz), a group of organisms that have the same traits and can produce offspring that can also produce offspring.

star, a ball of hot, glowing gases.

sternum (stėr′nəm), breastbone.

stratus (strā′təs) **cloud,** a cloud that forms in layers that spread across the sky.

subduction (səb′dək shən), the sliding of one of the earth's plates under another.

submersible (səb mėr′sə bəl), that which can be put under water.

subsonic (sub son′ik), having to do with speed less than the speed of sound.

supersonic (sü′pər son′ik), capable of moving faster than sound.

system (sis′təm), a group of organs that work together to do a job; a set of things or parts that form a whole and work together or affect one another.

T

temperate climate (tem′pər it klī′mit), a major climate zone that receives indirect sunlight in the winter and more direct sunlight in the summer.

theory (thē′ər ē), one or more related hypotheses supported by data that best explains things or events.

thermometer (thər mom′ə tər), an instrument for measuring temperature.

Acknowledgments

ScottForesman

Editorial: Terry Flohr, Janet Helenthal, Mary Ann Mortellaro, Kathleen Ludwig, Glen Phelan, Matthew Shimkus

Art and Design: Barbara Schneider, Jacqueline Kolb, George Roth, Cathy Sterrett

Picture Research/Photo Studio: Nina Page, Kelly Mountain, Judy Ladendorf, John Moore

Photo Lab/Keyline: Marilyn Sullivan, Mark Barberis, Gwen Plogman

Production: Barbara Albright, Francine Simon

Marketing: Lesa Scott, Ed Rock

Ligature, Inc.

Pupil Edition interior design and production

Unless otherwise acknowledged, all photographs are the property of ScottForesman. Unless otherwise acknowledged, all computer graphics by Ligature, Inc. Page abbreviations are as follows: **(T) top, (C) center, (B) bottom, (L) left, (R) right, (INS) inset.**

Module A
Photographs
Front & Back Cover: Background: "Constellations of the Northern Hemisphere" chart © Frank Schaffer Co., Frank Schaffer Publications Inc.   Children's Photos: John Moore

Page **A2,16,17,22,26,27,28,29,32,33,36,43,59(TL-INS), 60** NASA   **A3(T)** Jon Riley/Tony Stone Worldwide **A18,19(T)** A Mount Wilson & Palomar Observatory Photograph **A21(L)** National Optical Astronomy Observatories **A21(R)** National Optical Astronomy Observatories **A44-45(T)** Jon Riley/Tony Stone Worldwide   **A44-45(C)** Robin Smith/Tony Stone Worldwide   **A44-45(B)** Baron Wolman **A46** Jeff Schultz/Alaska Photo/All Stock   **A50(ALL)** William H. Amos   **A51** Anne Wertheim/ANIMALS ANIMALS **A53(T)** Don & Pat Valenti/f/Stop Pictures, Inc.   **A53(B)** Patrice Ceisel/Tom Stack & Associates   **A58** Courtesy of Stuart Elementary School, Patrick County, Virginia   **A59** Park Seed Company   **A59(TL)** NASA   **A62(L)** Don & Pat Valenti/f/Stop Pictures, Inc.   **A62(C)** Don and Pat Valenti   **A62(R)** Don & Pat Valenti/f/Stop Pictures, Inc.

Illustrations
Page **A5** Roberta Polfus   **A6-7** Roberta Polfus **A10-11** Roberta Polfus   **A18-19** George Kelvin **A34-35** Jacque Auger   **A34-35(INS)** Randy Verougstraete **A36** Jacque Auger   **A40** Nancy Lee Walter **A44** Roberta Polfus

Module B
Photographs
Front & Back Cover: Background: Paul Berger/Tony Stone Worldwide   Children's Photos: John Moore

Page **B5** E.R.Degginger   **B6-7** Mark Kelly/Alaska Stock Photo **B8(T)** Wolfgang Kaehler   **B13(R)** Hermann Eisenbeiss/ Photo Researchers   **B16(B)** Wolfgang Kaehler   **B24** Robert W. Blickensderfer/Ohio Sea Grant   **B25** Robert W.Blickensderfer **B30(R)** Ray Pfortner/Peter Arnold, Inc.   **B35(L)** Photo Researchers   **B36-37** Francois Gohier/Photo Researchers **B38(R)** Jack Dermid/Photo Researchers   **B39(L)** Scott Blackman/ Tom Stack & Associates   **B40-41** Robert C. Fields/Earth Scenes **B44-45** Baron Wolman   **B48** E.R.Degginger   **B51(L)** From BEHOLD MAN/Lennart Nilsson/Bonnier Fakta   **B51(R)** Steve Allen/Peter Arnold, Inc.   **B54-55** Carl Purcell/Photo Researchers **B58** Visuals Unlimited   **B59** Zig Leszczynski/ANIMALS ANIMALS   **B62(L)** Andrew J.Martinez   **B62(R)** Stephen Frink/Waterhouse   **B69** Bruce Robinson   **B70(L)** Andrew J. Martinez   **B70-71** Fred Bavendam/Peter Arnold, Inc.   **B71(INS)** Andrew J.Martinez   **B72** Visuals Unlimited   **B75** Visuals Unlimited **B76** Will Brown for ScottForesman

Illustrations
Page **B22-23** Joe Le Monnier   **B35** Charles Thomas **B37** Joe Le Monnier   **B38** Walter Stuart   **B44** JAK Graphics **B56-57** Walter Stuart   **B58-59** Cindy Brodie **B65** Walter Stuart   **B67** Walter Stuart   **B68** Walter Stuart **B77** George Kelvin

Module C
Photographs
Front & Back Cover: Background: Visuals Unlimited Children's Photos: John Moore

Page **C3(TL)** Reuters/UPI/Bettmann   **C3(B)** Paul Miller/Black Star   **C5(T)** Dave Millert/Tom Stack & Associates **C5(B)** Visuals Unlimited   **C7(T)** Ron Watts/Black Star **C14** Michael and Patricia Fogden   **C19** E.R.Degginger **C22(CR)** Stephen Dalton/Photo Researchers   **C25** Gary Braasch **C25(INS)** David Olson/Black Star   **C27** Reuters/UPI/Bettmann **C30** Peter Frenzen/U.S.Forestry Service   **C31(BL)** Jerry Franklin/U.S.Forestry Service   **C32** Gary Braasch **C32(INS)** Gary Braasch   **C34-35** David Olson/Black Star **C34(TC)** Thomas Kitchin/Tom Stack & Associates **C34(BC)** Gary Braasch   **C35(TC)** Peter K.Ziminski/Visuals Unlimited   **C35(BR)** Gary Braasch   **C36(C)** Tim Rock/Earth Scenes   **C36(B)** Anna E. Zuckerman/ Tom Stack & Associates **C40** William H.Amos   **C43** Reprinted Courtesy of H.M.Gousha/ Simon & Schuster   **C44** Visuals Unlimited   **C45** Visuals Unlimited   **C48** David Olson/Black Star   **C49** Paul Miller/ Black Star   **C49(INS)** Arnold Genthe/Library of Congress **C52(T)** NASA   **C58** Alfred Borcover   **C60** James E.Stoots, Jr./ Lawrence Livermore National Laboratory

Illustrations

Page **C2** Ebet Dudley   **C7** Ebet Dudley   **C8-9** Ebet Dudley
C12-13 Ebet Dudley   **C14-15** Joe Le Monnier   **C16-17** Joe Le
Monnier   **C18** Joe Le Monnier   **C18(INS)** Ebet Dudley
C22 Ebet Dudley   **C44-45** Ebet Dudley   **C48** Ebet Dudley
C50-51 Hank Iken   **C56** JAK Graphics   **C59** Rich Lo
C61 Rich Lo

Module D
Photographs
Front & Back Cover: Background: Kim Taylor/Bruce Coleman,
Inc.   Children's Photos: John Moore

Page **D3(ALL T)** Stephen Dalton/Photo Researchers
D3(BL) The Granger Collection, New York   **D5** Michael &
Patricia Fogden   **D21** Stephen Dalton/ANIMALS ANIMALS
D22(L) Stephen Dalton/Photo Researchers   **D24(L)** NOAA/
NESDIS/NCDC   **D24(R)** T.C.Kelley/Photo Researchers
D26-27 Tom McHugh/Photo Researchers   **D28** Kim Taylor/
Bruce Coleman, Inc.   **D32(T)** Frans Lanting/Minden Pictures
D34(L) Wendy Shattil and Bob Rozinski/Tom Stack & Associates
D35(B) Francois Gohier/Photo Researchers   **D38** Pat & Tom
Leeson/Photo Researchers   **D40** Richard Legeckis/Nesdid/
Rsmas/NOAA/NESDIS/NCDC   **D41** The Granger Collection,
New York   **D42(T)** Science Museum, London   **D44(T)** Greg
Vaughn/Tom Stack & Associates   **D44(B)** Haward Gallery
London, Tetva Associates   **D45(CR)** NASA   **D45(TC)** Library
of Congress   **D45(BC)** Library of Congress   **D50(T)** John
Covant/Photri, Inc.   **D52** NASA   **D53** NASA
D58(T) AP/Wide World   **D58(B)** M Barrett/H. Armstrong
Roberts   **D62(L)** Rod Planck/Tom Stack & Associates
D62(C) Stephen Dalton/ANIMALS ANIMALS
D62(R) Frans Lanting/ALLSTOCK,INC.
D67(ALL) E/NOAA/NESDIS/NCDC

Illustrations

Page **D5** Toni Goffe   **D6-7** Francisco Maruca
D8(T) Francisco Maruca   **D8(B)** Toni Goffe   **D24-25** Eric
Wright   **D28** Dickson O. Tabe   **D32-33** Kirk Caldwell
D34 Kirk Caldwell   **D35** Kirk Caldwell   **D42-43** Chris
Costello   **D50-51** Chris Costello   **D56** JAK Graphics
D58 JAK Graphics

Module E
Photographs
Front Cover: Children's Photos: John Moore

Page **E3(TL)** NOAA   **E3(TR)** Van Bucher/Photo Researchers
E3(B) Franca Principe, Instituto e Museo di Storra della Scienza,
Florence   **E15** Warren Faidley/Weatherstock   **E16** Wolfgang
Kaehler   **E22** Michael & Elvan Habicht/Earth Scenes
E23 Elvan Habicht/Peter Arnold, Inc.   **E24(L)** NOAA/NESDIS/
NCDC   **E29(L)** G.I.Bernard/Earth Scenes   **E29(R)** G.I.Bernard/
Earth Scenes   **E30(T)** James P. Jackson/Photo Researchers
E31 Gary Braasch/Alaska Photo Collection/ALLSTOCK
E37(L) Charlie Ott/Photo Researchers   **E37(R)** E.R.Degginger
E41 ERIM, Ann Arbor, MI   **E45** Richard Kolar/Earth Scenes
E46 Peter B.Kaplan/Photo Researchers   **E47(R)** Peter B.Kaplan/
Photo Researchers   **E48(T)** Mickey Gibson/Earth Scenes
E48(B) Peter Arnold, Inc.   **E49** Peter Arnold, Inc.
E50 E.R.Degginger   **E53** E.R.Degginger   **E54(T)** Bob
Daemmrich/Stock Boston   **E54(T INS)** Joyce Photographics/
Photo Researchers   **E54(B)** Richard Pasley/Stock Boston
E54(B INS) E.R.Degginger   **E55(T)** David Woodward/Tony
Stone Worldwide   **E55(T INS)** Gary Brettnacher/Tony Stone
Worldwide   **E55(B)** Sam C.Pierson/Photo Researchers

E55(B INS) Tony Freeman/Photo Edit   **E58** E.R.Degginger
E60 Franca Principe, Instituto e Museo di Storia della Scienza,
Florence   **E61** Van Bucher/Photo Researchers   **E62(T)** Photo
Researchers   **E62(B)** Stephen Frisch/Stock Boston   **E63** Tony
Stone Worldwide   **E75** E.R.Degginger

Illustrations

Page **E11** Joe Le Monnier   **E12-13** Joe Le Monnier
E14 Joe Le Monnier   **E17** Joe Le Monnier   **E32** Susan Nethery
E36-37 Greg McNair   **E38-39** Joe Le Monnier   **E57** Susan
Nethery   **E72** JAK Graphics   **E77** Gary Torrisi

Module F
Photographs
Front & Back Cover: Background: Victor Englebert   Children's
Photos: John Moore

Page **F2(BR)** Michael & Patricia Fogden   **F6** Victor Englebert
F14(T) Michael & Patricia Fogden   **F14(C)** Michael & Patricia
Fogden   **F14(B)** Jany Sauvamet/Photo Researchers
F19(L) Gary Retherford/Photo Researchers
F19(C) Jack Swenson/Tom Stack & Associates
F19(R) J.P. Varin/Jacana/Tom Stack & Associates
F24(C) NOAA/NESDIS/NCDC   **F25(L)** Rugerio Reis/Black
Star   **F25(R)** Walt Anderson/Visuals Unlimited   **F26** Victor
Englebert   **F28** Dan Brennan/Knut Bry   **F30(B)** Loren McIntyre
F40 John Cancalosi/Peter Arnold, Inc.   **F44(T)** Jane Thomas/
Visuals Unlimited   **F44(B)** Loren McIntyre   **F45(T)** Victor
Englebert   **F45(B)** George Loun/Visuals Unlimited
F59(T) E.R.Degginger   **F59(B)** Michael Fogden/Bruce Coleman,
Inc.   **F60** Courtesy University of Wisconsin

Illustrations

Page **F3** John Burgoyne   **F7** Mark Smith   **F8-9** Cindy Brodie
F10 John Burgoyne   **F14-15** John Burgoyne   **F28-29** Joe Le
Monnier   **F30** Joe Le Monnier   **F34-35** Wild Onion Studio
F36 Ebet Dudley   **F56** JAK Graphics   **F61** Wild Onion Studio
Leaf Borders throughout module (**F4, 5, 6, 7, 10, 11, 14, 16, 17,
18, 19, 24, 25, 28, 29, 30, 31, 34, 35, 42, 43, 46, 47, 50, 51,
52, 53**) by John Burgoyne

➤ *Many volcanoes are found around the Ring of Fire where plates are colliding.*

China

The Ring of Fire

There are about 500 active volcanoes on earth—volcanoes that have erupted in the past 50 years. More than 300 of them are found on the Ring of Fire. The Ring of Fire is a giant ring of volcanoes that surrounds the Pacific Plate.

The volcanoes on the Ring of Fire form where the huge moving plates collide. The picture at the bottom of the next page shows what can happen when one of these rocky plates slides under another plate. In the picture, the front edge of the left plate is sliding under the front edge of the right plate. As the left plate slides down into the earth, it enters the hot mantle. Rocks in the sliding plate begin to melt, and the melting rocks form magma. The magma then rises to the surface, and a volcano forms.

Australia

▲ **Volcanoes**
Ring of Fire

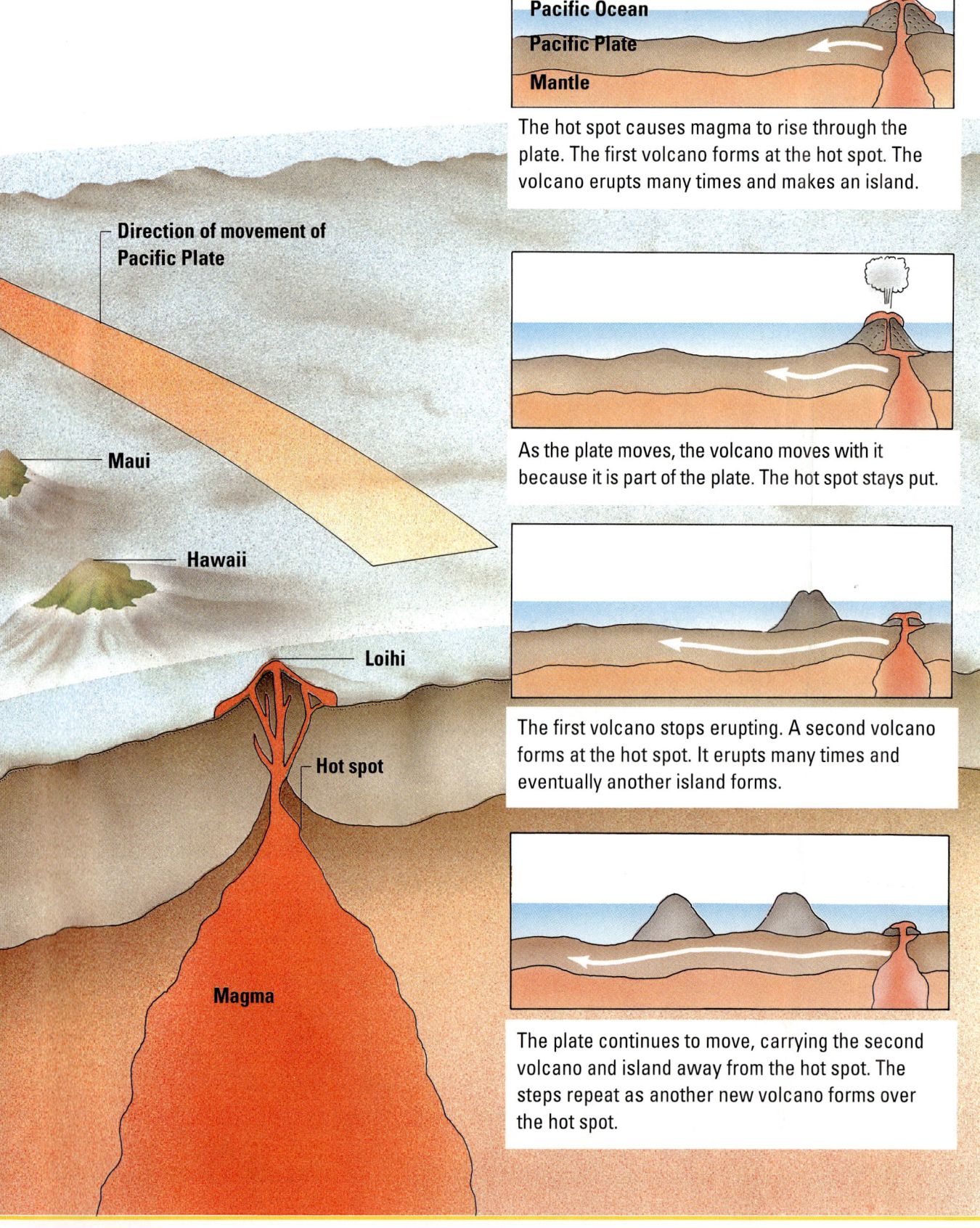

Direction of movement of Pacific Plate

Maui

Hawaii

Loihi

Hot spot

Magma

Pacific Ocean

Pacific Plate

Mantle

The hot spot causes magma to rise through the plate. The first volcano forms at the hot spot. The volcano erupts many times and makes an island.

As the plate moves, the volcano moves with it because it is part of the plate. The hot spot stays put.

The first volcano stops erupting. A second volcano forms at the hot spot. It erupts many times and eventually another island forms.

The plate continues to move, carrying the second volcano and island away from the hot spot. The steps repeat as another new volcano forms over the hot spot.

All in a Row

What happens when a hot spot stays put, but the crust above it keeps moving? A chain of islands forms!

Millions of years ago, a hot spot formed under the Pacific Plate. The hot spot melted the mantle and formed magma. The magma rose and formed a volcano. The volcano erupted many times and grew into an island.

Over many years, the Pacific Plate slowly moved away, but the hot spot stayed in the same place. A new volcano formed and grew into an island. As the plate continued moving, new volcanoes formed new islands. Over millions of years, the Hawaiian Islands formed. Today, a new volcano, Loihi, is growing over the hot spot. If it continues to grow, it will become a new Hawaiian Island.

Niihau · Kauai · Oahu · Molokai · Lanai · Kahoolawe · Pacific Ocean · Pacific Plate · Mantle

Each plate drifts between 1 and 10 centimeters every year across the upper layer of the mantle, which is made of partly melted rock. Most scientists think that the plates move because of convection currents, as shown in the picture below.

In a convection current, differences in temperature force material to move in a circular pattern. Hot material rises, while cold material sinks. In the earth's mantle, hot magma rises up to the plates and spreads out sideways. The spreading magma acts like a conveyor belt and carries the plates along. As the magma spreads, it cools. The cool magma then sinks back into the mantle, where it heats and rises again.

Convection currents in the mantle sometimes bring magma up to where two plates meet. The magma pushes the plates apart as it melts through the weak area between them, forming a volcano.

Although many volcanoes form along plate boundaries, some form over what are called hot spots. Hot spots are areas, within the mantle, of extreme heat and melting action. The Hawaiian Islands formed as the Pacific Plate moved over a hot spot in the mantle.

▼ Circular convection currents in the mantle may cause the plates to move.

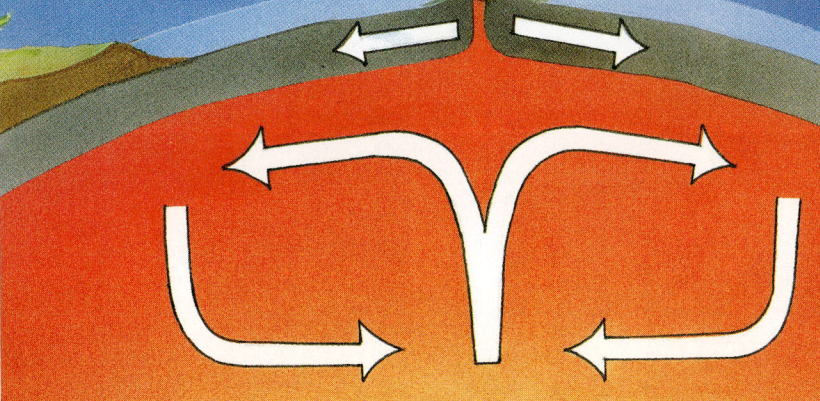